A PANORAMA OF THE BIBLE

LAY ACTION MINISTRY PROGRAM
5827 S. RAPP ST.
LITTLETON, CO 80120

DAVID C. COOK PUBLISHING CO.
850 N. GROVE AVE.
ELGIN, IL 60120

A Panorama of the Bible © 1988 by Lay Action Ministry Program, Inc.

Scripture quotations, unless otherwise noted, are taken from the HOLY BIBLE, NEW INTERNATIONAL VERSION, © 1973, 1978, 1984 International Bible Society. Used by permission of Zondervan Bible Publishers.

David C. Cook Publishing Co.
850 North Grove Avenue
Elgin, IL 60120
Printed in U.S.A

Editor: Gary Wilde
Designer: Chris Patchel
Cover: Lois Rosio Sprague

ISBN: 0-89191-511-7
Library of Congress Catalog Number: 87-72833

TABLE OF
CONTENTS

LAY ACTION
MINISTRY PROGRAM

LAMP courses are based on the HEAD, HEART, and HANDS approach to learning. HEAD represents Bible *content* that you want to know. HEART represents your *personal application* of the truth. HANDS refers to the LAMP goal of preparing you to *use content in the lives of other people*—imparting to others what you have learned (see II Tim. 2:2).

A Panorama of the Bible seeks to fulfill the LAMP goals by helping participants get a grasp of the Bible as a totality—the whole flow of Biblical history at their fingertips. They will do this by studying, in survey fashion, each period of Biblical history, then memorizing a symbol that pulls together the major events and personalities within that period. Also, each chapter focuses upon a life issue of that period which has relevance for practical Christian growth today.

How to Use This Course

This course is for every Christian who is willing to put forth the effort in personal study. But we want you to know "up front" what it is going to cost you in terms of time and commitment. First, *it is going to cost you a good hour of home study for each lesson*. Make every effort to spend this much time as a minimum requirement.

Though you may complete the course by yourself, you will normally be preparing for a weekly group meeting. In this meeting you will be an active participant because of your personal study. One lesson is to be completed each week, prior to coming to the weekly group meeting.

The group meeting features a discussion of the lesson that you have studied during the week. It also includes other elements to encourage group life, and to guide group members toward personal application of the material. The meeting, planned for at least a full hour, should be led by a person who enjoys leading discussions and helping people learn. The study leader will study the lesson in the same way as anyone else in the group, with the aid of the four-step lesson plans at the back of the book. In addition, a fuller, more detailed Leader's Guide can be obtained from:

DAVID C. COOK PUBLISHING CO.
850 NORTH GROVE AVENUE
ELGIN, IL 60120

or:
LAY ACTION MINISTRY PROGRAM, INC.
5827 S. RAPP STREET
LITTLETON, CO 80120

A Panorama
Of the Bible

Mountain climbers love their sport. For them, nothing can compare with the exhilaration and sense of accomplishment derived from reaching a lofty summit.

Becoming well acquainted with the Bible is similar to mountain climbing. It takes determination. As you study this course, like climbing a mountain, you will attain higher and higher goals until you are able to view the grand panorama of God's Word.

Learning twelve simple visual symbols will enable you to remember the twelve periods of Bible history. Notice that the circle symbols represent God's creation. The rectangle in the next eight symbols represents Israel, God's channel for the Messiah. The Cross in the last two symbols represents Christ's Gospel age.

Take a few minutes now to study the symbols.

Twelve Periods of
Bible History

 1. BEGINNING. Creation of the heavens (cloud) and earth (circle).

 2. PATRIARCHS. Four partriarchal persons are represented by four intertwined circles.

 3. EXODUS. The nation Israel is formed. (The four circles become a rectangle that hereafter

represents Israel.) Arrows represent Israel's departure from Egypt.

4. SETTLEMENT. The nation enters, conquers, and divides the Promised Land. (Imagine the two rectangles of #3 and #4 as rockets making exit and entry.)

5. JUDGES. Israel is suppressed (dark cloud) by other nations, and boundaries disappear (broken line).

6. UNITED KINGDOM. The kingdom is united under a king (crown).

7. DIVIDED KINGDOM. The kingdom is divided between the northern kingdom of Israel and the southern kingdom of Judah (represented by the torn rectangle and broken crown).

8. CAPTIVITY. Assyria scatters Israel, and Babylonia carries Judah into exile.

9. RESTORATION. Persia now rules the world, and allows Judah to return to restore Jerusalem.

10. SILENT YEARS. The intertestamental years are represented by brackets (only the ends of a rectangle).

11. CHRIST. Jesus Christ comes as the world's Messiah, represented by the Cross.

12. CHURCH. Christ's Church is a new people comprised of Jews and Gentiles.

PERIOD ONE:
BEGINNINGS

This is the symbol that identifies the first of twelve great periods in Bible history. We have given the name of that period **BEGINNINGS**. The Book of Genesis, the first book in the Bible, emphasizes "birth," "generation," or "beginnings." This phrase is repeated numerous times in the book. Therefore the Book of Genesis is the Book of Beginnings.

The key words in each lesson are in **BOLD** type, such as **GENESIS 1—11** below. You will be asked to remember these **BOLD** printed words at the end of each lesson.

Some of the important things which began in **GENESIS 1—11** are: Creation (1:1, 8, 10, 14, 24); the human race (1:26, 27; 2:7); the Sabbath (2:2, 3); marriage (2:18, 21-25); sin (3:1-7); sacrifice (3:21; 4:4; 8:20); family life (4:1, 2); death (2:17; 4:8); godless civilization (4:16, 17; 11:4); nations (10:5, 32) languages (11:6-9); and redemptive revelation (3:15).

Creation

God's **CREATION** of the universe is the first of the key events of the first period. Notice the order of God's Creation on the Creation days. How does this order compare with modern science, which teaches that life began with very simple life forms and gradually became more complex, until finally human beings appeared on earth?

_____

_____

True science and the Bible must ultimately agree. Why?

_____

What was it about the creation of humans that made them essentially different from the rest of Creation (Gen. 1:26, 27)?

_____

What does this imply about the responsibility of humankind?

_____

The creation of mankind (male and female) towers over the rest of creation, since they were created "in the image of God." Thus we have characteristics like those of God—in relation to purpose, moral consciousness, and responsibility. Mankind is capable of having fellowship with God in holiness and in love.

What evidence is there that humans were intelligent beings from the time of their creation (Gen. 1:26, 27; 2:7, 20)?

_____

The emphasis of Genesis 1—11 is upon the sin and moral corruption of humankind. After their creation, people's repeated rebellions caused three great judgments: the Fall; the Flood; and Babel.

Fall

In the FALL man and woman sinned against God and were cast out of Eden, where God had placed them in an ideal environment. Through this act of disobedience, sin passed upon all humankind (Rom. 5:12).

In the story of the Fall we have an opportunity to

examine Satan's technique. How did he make his appearance? (Gen. 3:1; see also Rev. 12:9)

_____

Whose word did he question? (Gen. 3:1) _____

To what did he appeal? (Gen. 3:5) _____

What are the three aspects of temptation? (Compare Gen. 3:6 with I Jn. 2:16.)

_____

_____

Describe how this information is helpful in your life.

_____

_____

List the results of Satan's evil work in the lives of Adam and Eve, as found in Genesis 3:7, 8?

_____

_____

What were additional effects on Eve? (Gen. 3:16)

_____

What were additional effects on Adam? (Gen. 3:17-19)

_____

The effect of Adam's and Eve's sin went far beyond their own lives. The difference in human nature after the Fall is seen in Cain, who became jealous and killed his brother Abel (Gen. 4:1-8). And that was just the beginning of wickedness! What did God conclude about human sinfulness in Genesis 6:5?

_____

The great wickedness of humankind eventually resulted in the Flood, wherein humankind was washed from the face of the earth. What statement by God, in

Genesis 8:21, shows that people's sinful nature was not changed, even after the Flood?

Flood

The world had become exceedingly corrupt by Noah's time. God sent the FLOOD to stem the tide of sinfulness. God had shown mercy through 120 years of forewarning. Noah was commanded to build a large ark that would provide safety for him and his family. Pairs, and sometimes sevens of animals, were brought into the ark. All the descendants of Cain were destroyed in the Flood, as well as most of the descendants of Seth; and God made a new beginning. The Flood stands as a powerful object lesson of God's ultimate judgment upon all sin, and our need of redemption. But the ark symbolizes God's provision of a way of escape—salvation by grace.

Babel

As humankind multiplied after the Flood, Noah's sons, Shem, Ham, and Japheth, settled in different parts of the world, and became fathers of three divisions of humanity. One of Shem's descendants was Abraham, founder of the Hebrew nation. The race of Ham produced Nimrod, the rebellious founder of the tower of BABEL. What reason did the people give for attempting to build the tower of Babel? (Gen. 11:4)

How did this reason compare with God's will in Genesis 1:28?

What two things did God do to put an end to the building of this tower? (Gen. 11:5-9)

_____

_____

The tower of Babel may have inspired the Ziggurats of ancient Babylon. The Ziggurat was a pyramid-type structure, spiraled by a ramp and topped by a temple, in which some form of astrology or sun worship was apparently carried out.

Learning About Sin

The Bible begins with a strong emphasis on the creaturehood of human beings, thereby emphasizing their inherent worth and value before God. This is the basis for all self-esteem that we may ever have. As a small child once put it: "God made me, and God don't make no junk!"

But the first book of the Bible also immediately focuses upon the sin and depravity that entered the human race. The New Testament strongly emphasizes sin as well. Accepting our sinfulness is necessary in order to show us our deep need for a Savior. Such a recognition spurs us to put our faith in Christ as Savior and Lord.

This teaching of the universality of sin is clearly taught by Paul in his Letter to the Romans. How does God react, in Romans 1:18-32, to the "godlessness and wickedness of men who suppress the truth by their wickedness"?

_____

In many ways this looks quite modern, doesn't it? Write down aspects of Paul's description of humanity in Romans 1:18-32 that you see in society today.

_____

_____

_____

In Romans 2 Paul speaks to the supposed "righteous." What statement does he make about them? (Rom. 2:1)

_____

He concludes, in Romans 3:9-18, with a literal volley of Scripture, effectively sinking any remaining idea that persons, through their own efforts, could become righteous in God's sight. The ongoing sin problem, Paul states, is that in sinning, Adam's very nature was changed. Further, this change was transmitted to all members of the human race. ("Therefore, just as sin entered the world through one man, and death through sin, and in this way death came to all men, because all sinned—" Rom. 5:12.)

God created us to have fellowship with Him. But through disobedience, fellowship with God was broken (Gen. 3:8, 22-24). The Bible later calls this separation spiritual death. Read Ephesians 2:1-3 in at least two Bible translations. Then, describe in your own words this spiritual condition of fallen humanity.

_____

_____

The practical significance of this truth is all-important. We must see our spiritual condition as God sees it. Next examine Ephesians 2:4-10. How did God demonstrate His love for us? (Eph. 2:4-7; see also Rom. 5:8)

_____

How are we to respond to that provision? (Eph. 2:8, 9; see also Jn. 1:12)

_____

With what results in our lives? (Eph. 2:10)

_____

Symbol for Period One
Take a moment to review the basic symbol found at the

14

beginning of this chapter. Then, memorize the added items (on the symbol at the left) that will enable you to recall the four key events that took place during period one.

The first arrow represents God's work of _____ _____ . The second arrow represents man on earth, losing his innocent estate in the _____ . The third arrow represents the _____ that rose and covered the earth in judgment. The fourth arrow represents human effort to build a tower at _____ that would rise to the heavens for humankind's glory.

Check out these aids for remembering these symbols. The first arrow represents God reaching down, in His work of **CREATION**. The second arrow represents humankind on earth, losing its innocent estate in the **FALL**. The third arrow represents the **FLOOD** that rose and covered the earth in judgment. The fourth arrow represents the effort to build a tower at **BABEL** that would rise to the heavens for humankind's glory.

For period one, you now should have fixed in your mind the complete symbol, the name of the period, its Bible location, and the words for the key events.

Now. Are you ready for your personal quiz over this period? Cover up the preceding material. Draw, in the box below, the complete symbol from memory. Also write the name of the period, the Bible location (see the Table of Contents for this), and each of the key words.

Complete symbol	Period name: _____
	Bible location: _____
	Key words:
	_____
	_____
	_____
	_____

2

PERIOD TWO:
PATRIARCHS

This symbol identifies the second period of Bible history. We call this the period of the **PATRIARCHS**.

"Patriarch" was the title given a paternal leader of a family or tribe. The term applies generally to persons whose names appear in the genealogies prior to Moses. More particularly however, it refers to Abraham, Isaac, Jacob, Joseph, and his brothers (the heads of the tribes of Israel).

GENESIS 12—50 records the history of these four patriarchs. Whereas Genesis 1—11 focuses on four *events*, the remainder of Genesis focuses on four *persons:* Abraham, in Genesis 12—23, Isaac in Genesis 24-27, Jacob in Genesis 28—36, and Joseph in Genesis 37—50.

Abraham

Around 2000 B.C. God called **ABRAHAM**, first named Abram, to leave his homeland in Ur and travel 1,000 miles to a new and strange country. Skim Genesis 12, where God makes some very special promises to the childless Abraham. What did God promise him in regard to:

1. A nation? (Gen. 12:2)

2. Relationships with other nations? (Gen. 12:3)

_____

3. A land? (Gen. 12:7)

_____

Abraham began this journey with his father, Terah, and brother Nahor and their families, and traveled as far as Haran (Gen. 11:29-32).

After his father died, Abraham again heard God's call to go to Canaan (Acts 7:2-4), and he obeyed. Traveling with Abraham was his entire household, including his nephew Lot. Traveling slowly with their sheep and other animals, the trip may have taken as long as several years.

There was fairly constant bickering between the herdsmen of Lot and those of Abraham. This finally resulted in the two groups going their separate ways. Lot then moved his home near the city of Sodom and became identified with these vile people (see chap. 13). Later, Abraham was forced to rescue him in a pitched battle with neighboring kings (chap. 14). Even after being delivered from the destruction of Sodom, Lot's daughters promoted an incestuous relationship with their father (19:30-38).

Abraham did not always walk uprightly before the Lord either. He went into Egypt, where he deceived Pharaoh (12:10-20); he took Hagar as his wife, instead of waiting for God's promise (16:1-4); he doubted God (17:17); and he went a second time into Egypt where he again compromised truth (chap. 20).

In what ways are Abraham's shortcomings an encouragement to you?

_____

_____

_____

_____

Dominant in the Book of Genesis, however, are the many examples of Abraham's godly character and faith:

- He believed God when he left for Canaan (12:1-9).
- He showed godly character in separating from Lot (13:5-13).
- He tithed all of his earthly possessions to Melchizedek (14:17-24).
- He was a man of prayer (13:3,4; 18:22-33).
- He trusted God even in the offering of his son Isaac (chap. 22).

Isaac

Because Sarah was old and past the age of childbearing, she persuaded Abraham to have a child by her handmaid, Hagar. But God told Abraham that Hagar's son, Ishmael, would not be the child through whom the chosen nation would develop. Instead, God promised to do a miraculous thing in giving Sarah a son, ISAAC, who would be the child of the promise. Isaac was born to Sarah when she was 90 years old and Abraham was 100. Through Isaac, Sarah became the "mother of nations" (Gen. 17:16).

Isaac grew up a very special child indeed. The story of Abraham's provision for a bride for Isaac is fascinating and exciting. You can read about it in Genesis 24. This is a beautiful chapter with numerous lessons of God's gracious guidance through prayer and circumstances. Rebekah consented to become Isaac's wife and undertook the long journey back to Canaan.

Jacob

To Rebekah were born twins, Esau and JACOB. Jacob's name means "the supplanter." Jacob displaced his older brother Esau in a number of instances. Esau agreed to sell his birthright to Jacob. Later, Jacob deceived his father into giving him the blessing that belonged to Esau. After fleeing from Esau, Jacob came to Bethel, where God confirmed to him the covenant that He had made with Abraham and Isaac (28:11-19). Jacob settled in the land of Haran, where he worked for Laban and married Laban's two daughters, Leah and Rachel.

Despite his many faults, Jacob valued God's covenant blessings. After being chastened for his sin, Jacob developed into a man of God. On his return to Canaan, he wrestled with an angel at Bethel and his name was changed to Israel, because he "struggled with God and with men and have overcome" (Gen. 32:28). Jacob had twelve sons, from whom the twelve tribes of Israel descended.

Joseph

The most prominent son of Jacob was **JOSEPH**, upon whom a quarter of the Book of Genesis (37—50) centers. Detested by his brothers, Joseph was sold as a slave into Egypt. Among other things, Joseph's life shows that God is able to deliver the believer out of temptation. God took care of Joseph because he honored God. His integrity and faith proved strong, even in adverse circumstances.

In God's providence, Joseph was eventually promoted to become prime minister of Egypt. During a great famine he brought his father and the family clan into Egypt. He provided land for them in Goshen. There they grew from 70 to 600,000 men (Ex. 12:37), and developed the national strength needed to later take possession of the promised land of Canaan.

Fill in the featured members of God's "family tree" from this period, starting with Abraham and his wife Sarah.

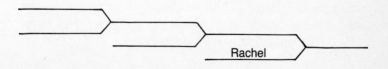

Learning About Faith

The life of Abraham is of profound importance to every Christian. Look first at the incident recorded in Genesis 15. Following Abraham's battle to rescue Lot, he quite naturally feared a possible counterattack.
Notice in verse 1, God's special promise to him. What great concern did Abraham express to God in verses 2 and 3?

God then gave Abraham two great promises. First, that Abraham's own son would be his heir. Second, that his descendants would be like the stars in number. What was Abraham's response to God's promise in Genesis 15:6? _____
Notice the wonderful statement that follows: "and [God] credited it to him as righteousness."

In all of the Bible there is no more important principle for our lives than this: God credited righteousness to Abraham *by faith alone.* So important is this truth about him that Paul devoted the entire fourth chapter of Romans to it.

Turn to Romans 4 now. How does Paul answer the question of how Abraham was made righteous, or justified? (4:1-5)

What does this mean for all people? (Rom. 4:4, 5)

This truth is also taught elsewhere in Paul's writings. In Galatians 3:6-9 Paul states that faith, and not law-keeping, is essential for anyone who wants a right relationship with God.

The exact nature of the relationship of works to the clear Biblical teaching of salvation by grace has been debated throughout church history.

How does James 2:22-24 say Abraham was justified?

_____

The apparent contradiction between Paul and James disappears as we examine James 2 more carefully. Notice first that James also quotes Genesis 15:6. Thus it is hardly likely that he would say something in direct conflict with this revealed truth!

Further, notice that James is dealing with a different set of values than was Paul. What kind of faith is James talking about in James 2:14-16, 19?

_____

How does this kind of faith compare with Abraham's?

_____

Thus, we may summarize by saying that James speaks to the fact that true faith is a faith that works. Works do not save us, but the saving _kind_ of faith will surely result in a life-style that grows in holiness.

Time out! May I ask you an important question? Have you placed your faith in Christ alone for your salvation as Paul teaches? _____ In the event you have not, you may do so by simply inviting Christ into your life to be your Savior and Lord. Be sure to talk to your study leader about this vital decision.

Now reflect on the evidences of your faith that James talks about. List some of these in the space below.

_____

_____

_____

Symbol for Period Two

(A)(I)(J)(J) Take a moment to review the basic symbol found at the beginning of this chapter. Then, memorize the added items (on the symbol at the left) that will enable you to recall the four key persons of period two.

Can you name the person whom each letter represents? You will remember that they are printed in BOLD type in each lesson.

A _____ I _____ J _____ J _____

The first two patriarchs were Abraham and Isaac. To remember the four letters, note their alphabetical order: A-I-J-J. That even applies to the last two, Jacob and Joseph. All are in father-son order.

Now, here's the test. After covering up the preceding material, draw the complete symbol for period two from memory. Also write in the period name, the Bible location, and the key words.

Complete symbol	Period name: _____
	Bible location: _____
	Key words:
	_____
	_____
	_____

_____

Great! Now you are ready for the group discussion.

PERIOD THREE:
EXODUS

 This is the symbol that identifies the third period in Bible history. We have given it the name EXODUS.

God's deliverance of Israel from Egypt illustrates the struggles of every person who seeks deliverance from the entangling influence of the world. It reveals God's power to deliver us from sin.

During Israel's stay in Egypt, the 12 tribes developed into a distinct nation. Their theocratic culture was established. They developed skills that they would later need in their long years of travel and wandering. God was preparing them for the Promised Land.

The conditions Israel experienced in Egypt changed from those of Joseph's day. What was the relationship of Israel to the new king in Egypt (Ex. 1:8-11)?

The Egyptians feared the increased power of the Israelites and therefore they enslaved them. God prepared Israel in the crucible of Egyptian bondage and then brought her out of Egypt with a mighty deliverance.

Exodus and Numbers

The history of the Israelites from the time of their

oppression in Egypt until they occupied Canaan is presented in the Books of **EXODUS** and **NUMBERS**. Leviticus and Deuteronomy also cover this same period, but from another point of view. Leviticus presents ceremonies prescribed by God at the end of the period covered by Exodus. Deuteronomy presents spiritual lessons as Moses restates the Law.

You will need a Bible map of the area shown below in order to complete the following exercise. If your Bible does not contain a set of maps, look for them in a Bible atlas, or in a Bible dictionary.

Write in the following five names in the appropriate spaces in the map below: Ezion Geber; Kadesh Barnea; Moab; Mt. Sinai; Rameses.

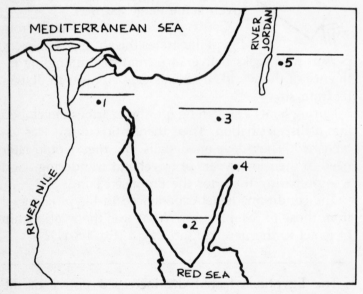

Next, draw a line showing the route the Israelites took in their journey from Rameses to Moab.

The major events and movements of Israel during this third period are as follows:

EVENTS	PLACE	SCRIPTURE
Moses' call, plagues, passover	At #1	Exodus 1—13

Red Sea crossing and journey	From #1 to 2	Exodus 14—18
Law, tabernacle, ceremonies	At #2	Exodus 19—40 Leviticus Numbers 1—10
Spying out the land	From #2 to 3	Numbers 11—14
Wanderings (38 years)	From #3 to 4 to 5	Numbers 15—33
Moses' last discourses & death	At #5	Deuteronomy

Now let's look at these events as Israel moved from Egypt (1), to Moab (5).

Moses

During this dark period, Pharaoh had Israel's innocent boy babies thrown into the Nile to prevent a further increase in their numbers. MOSES, however, was hidden by his mother. Later he was discovered by Pharaoh's own daughter, of all people. Moses grew up in the palace and was trained as a royal son.

When Moses was 40 years old, he attempted to protect his people against their oppressors. He killed a man in the process, and fled to the wilderness of Sinai, where he became a shepherd.

After 40 years in the desert, God called Moses to deliver His people. How did Moses respond? (Ex. 4:1, 10)

_____

_____

How did God answer his excuse? (vss. 11, 12)

_____

Does this story have a familiar ring? Does it sound like an echo from your own past? It sometimes seems easier to say "I can't" than to serve God. But if God is calling you to do a particular task, you can be sure that He will also enable you to do it. It is just as important for you to obey as it was for Moses.

Plagues

With Aaron as his spokesman, Moses demanded of Pharaoh, "Let my people go!" When Pharaoh refused, God showed His mighty power through the ten PLAGUES. The plagues increased in intensity while Pharaoh braced his stubborn heart against God. Briefly list the ten plagues recorded in the Book of Exodus.

1. 7:20, 21 _____
2. 8:5 _____
3. 8:17 _____
4. 8:21 _____
5. 9:3-7 _____
6. 9:10 _____
7. 9:23-25 _____
8. 10:12-15 _____
9. 10:21-23 _____
10. 11:4-7 _____

Many plagues were directed against Egyptian deities, showing God's complete power over them. For example, Hapi was the Nile god; Hequit was symbolized in the frog; and Ra, was the sun god. Compare Exodus 12:12; 18:10, 11 and Numbers 33:4.

Passover

In the last plague, a death angel struck all the first-born males of Egypt, but God delivered Israel's first-born in the PASSOVER. You can read about the offering of the sacrificial lamb in Exodus 12. The death angel "passed over" all homes where the lamb's blood was applied. The Passover is a picture of what provision of God for us? (see Mt. 26:19 with verses 26-28; and I Cor. 5:7)

_____

Christ is "the Lamb of God who takes away the sin of the world" (Jn. 1:29). He provided the all-sufficient sacrifice for our sins (Hebrews 9:27, 28; 10:10-14).

Parting of the Red Sea

Pharaoh first consented to let Israel go. Later he changed his mind, sending his army in hot pursuit. The miraculous PARTING OF THE RED SEA brought Israel to safety, while the Egyptians were drowned in the engulfing waters. The Exodus of the Israelites from Egypt gives us an all-time great picture of how God delivers His people from sin and destruction in the world.

Law

After crossing the Red Sea, Israel then journeyed to Mount Sinai, where God gave the LAW to Moses. When God gave the Ten Commandments to Moses, His voice must have echoed throughout the valley (compare Ex. 20:1, 18, 19). Read these familiar Commandments from Exodus 20:2-17; then briefly restate each in your own words.

The first four Commandments—our duty to God:

1. _____

2. _____

3. _____

4. _____

The final six Commandments—our duty to our neighbor:

5. _____

6. _____

7. _____

8. _____

9. _____

10. _____

The Ten Commandments are an expression of the holy character of God Himself. His standard of living for all people is seen in these laws. They are abiding principles that establish order in life and declare God's lordship over His people. God is holy; He requires that His people be holy, too. Moses later expanded these moral laws and added other regulations to guide the Israelites in their daily conduct.

Tabernacle

While Israel was at Sinai, God established for them a special way to worship Him. The movable place of worship and the priesthood were two main parts of this system. God's instructions for the TABERNACLE were given to Moses while he was on Mt. Sinai. The people then gladly contributed time, talent, and possessions to complete this center for worship.

The tribe of Levi was chosen to care for the Tabernacle. Aaron's family was appointed to serve as priests. They had charge of the sacrifices and represented the people before God. Hebrews 9 makes it clear that the Tabernacle is an illustration of Christ's atoning sacrifice for our sins.

Ceremonies

Completion of the Tabernacle made possible the use of elaborate CEREMONIES by which the people could approach God in worship.

Many Christians believe that the various sacrifices detailed in Leviticus 1—22 symbolize the Person and work of the Lord Jesus Christ who gave His life as our atoning sacrifice. He paid the complete penalty for the broken Law.

The appointed feasts (Lev. 23—27) kept alive certain important facts concerning the nation's existence, from the redemptive action of God in the Passover to a future day when God would dwell among them in person.

Wanderings

The Book of Numbers traces Israel's WANDERINGS after Sinai. At Kadesh Barnea, twelve men, one from each of the twelve tribes were sent to spy out the land of Canaan.

What was the negative report that ten of the spies brought back? (Num. 13:32, 33)

_____

_____

Who were the two spies who encouraged the people to enter the land? (Num. 14:6-9)

_____

What judgment did God pass upon Israel because of her unbelief? (Num. 14:26-34)

_____

For her unbelief and disobedience, Israel spent another 38 years of wandering. All those at Kadesh over 20 years old, except Joshua and Caleb, died without seeing the Promised Land. Only their children lived to enter and enjoy it. The faith of Joshua and Caleb is a great example for us to follow in our lives today.

Deuteronomy reviews the laws and encourages and warns Israel prior to her entry into Canaan and the end of the 40 years of wandering. This brings to a close the five books of Moses, referred to in Luke 24:44 as "the Law of Moses."

The Christian's Relationship to the Law

The relationship of Christians today to the Law of Moses is not always clearly understood. Romans and Galatians give us some insight about this relationship.

1. How does Paul illustrate the believer's relationship to the Law in Romans 7:1-3?

_____

2. How does that apply to the Christian and the Law? (Rom. 7:4-6)

_____

3. How, then, does the Christian properly relate to the Law? (Rom. 8:4)

_____

4. What does Paul say about those who rely on the law for their salvation? (Gal. 3:10; 4:21-23; 5:1-4)

_____

5. What is the purpose of the Law according to:

Romans 3:19, 20? _____

Galatians 3:24? _____

Symbol for Period Three

Take a moment to review the basic symbol found at the beginning of this chapter. Then, memorize the added items (on the symbol at the left) that will enable you to recall the key words of the period. Can you name the words that the items represent? Try.

M _____ ; P _____ ;
P _____ ; P _____ ;
L _____ ; T _____ ;
C _____ ; W _____ .

The first letter represents **MOSES**, the great leader of the Exodus. The three arrows represent three "P's" that were vital phases of the Exodus—**PLAGUES, PASSOVER, PARTING OF THE RED SEA.**

Within the rectangle are four simple drawings that represent these aspects of the wilderness journey—the giving of the **LAW** (two stone tablets side by side), the **TABERNACLE** (a tent), the **CEREMONIES** (an altar), and the wilderness **WANDERINGS** (broken line like footsteps that form a W). Take a few moments now to visualize each part of this symbol.

Now cover up the preceding material and draw the symbol for period three from memory, identify the period, Bible location, and key words.

Complete symbol	Period name: _____
	Bible location: _____
	Key words:
	_____
	_____
	_____

_____

_____

_____

_____

_____

PERIOD FOUR:
SETTLEMENT

 This is the symbol for period four: **SETTLEMENT.** Having surveyed the first three periods of Bible history, are you now ready for a military adventure? That's right, a military adventure, because in the fourth period we find ourselves in the company of Joshua and the men of Israel as they invade Canaan and blitz its territories. Their objective? To claim and settle Canaan as their God-given land.

Canaan was made up of a number of independent city-states that frequently were at war with one another. Their religious rites included many degrading practices—such as child sacrifice, idol worship, and prostitution. Israel's conquest was God's judgment against Canaan's deep moral corruption.

Joshua: The Book

Period four is covered in the Book of **JOSHUA.** It covers a period of 30 years. God's faithfulness to fulfill His promise is seen in His provision of the land of Canaan for the people of Israel. Israel now would have her own land and would be a true nation for the first time.

Joshua: The Man

Following Moses' death, Joshua was used of God to

fulfill His promise to bring Israel into Canaan. Joshua's name means "Jehovah is salvation." Its New Testament equivalent is the name *Jesus*. Joshua was a man of great spiritual power, courage, faith, prayer, and leadership. Just as Moses had led Israel out of bondage, Joshua now led her into the Promised Land. Turn now to Joshua 1 in your Bible. What was Joshua's relationship to Moses? (vs. 1)

_____

What was God's promise to Joshua? (in vss. 3 and 4)

_____

_____

In verse 5? _____

What was Joshua's responsibility? (vs. 6)

_____

In verse 7? _____

Verse 8 is a wonderful verse to guide your life. Look at it again. "Do not let this Book of the Law depart from your _____ ; _____ on it day and night, so that you may be careful to ____ everything written in it. Then you will be _____ and _____ ."

God calls all of us to some ministry or leadership in His work. This is a great honor, as well as a responsibility. How can we become effectively involved in God's work? One way is by working with and learning from one of God's servants. This was Joshua's approach, and it worked well for him. Paul sets forth this principle when he says, "Follow my example, as I follow the example of Christ" (I Cor. 11:1).

Jordan Crossing

Two spies were first sent to Jericho. They were protected there by the harlot Rahab, who, in Hebrews 11:31 and James 2:25 is mentioned favorably as an example of a woman who had faith in God. What impor-

33

tant information did Rahab give the spies? (Josh. 2:8-11)

_____

_____

The **JORDAN CROSSING** was the same kind of miracle that God performed for Israel at the beginning of her exodus from Egypt. Now, 40 years later, and for a new generation, God again parted the waters as Israel was led across the Jordan on dry ground. The Ark of the Covenant, carried by the Levites, led the way. While the priests stood with the ark in the middle of the river, the people crossed over (chap. 3). Stones to memorialize the occasion were erected both in Gilgal and in the midst of the river (chap. 4).

What effect did this crossing have on the Canaanites? (5:1)

_____

While camped at Gilgal near Jericho, Joshua admonished the people regarding their covenant relationship to God, thus preparing them for the conquest. The ordinance of circumcision was there renewed. The Passover was observed for the first time in the land of Canaan. The manna that had been furnished throughout the wilderness journey now ceased and the Israelites began to live off the produce of the land of Canaan.

Conquer

Under the guidance of God Himself, the Captain of Salvation, Joshua led Israel to **CONQUER** the land of Canaan. The successful conquest of Canaan in three brilliant campaigns makes exciting reading. The first campaign began with the conquering of Jericho. This drove a wedge into the center of Canaan, and divided the land in two. By dividing the northern enemies from those in the south, Joshua prevented a united, land-wide coalition.

No actual fighting was done to conquer Jericho. What might have appeared to be a foolish parade was the method God used to show that He was the One who gained the victory. How does Hebrews 11:30 say the walls of Jericho fell?

_____

Amazing! What are some of the ways our faith can be used? (Incorporate I Jn. 5:4; Heb. 11:1, 2 and Eph. 6:16 in your response.)

_____

Careful instructions had been given concerning the disposition of the spoils of Jericho (Josh. 6:18). What was the sin of the soldier named Achan? (see Josh. 7:1, 19-21)

_____

Notice the four steps that led to Achan's sin, as indicated in his confession in Joshua 7:21. These were: 1) _____ 2) _____ 3) _____ 4) _____ . How does this compare with the sin of his original parents in the Garden of Eden? (see Genesis 3:6-8)

_____

Achan's sin also shows the effect one person's disobedience can have on all the people of God. Through his personal sin, Achan brought defeat to all of Israel at the hands of the relatively small city of Ai. Only after Achan's sin was judged did God again give victory to Israel. What principle might this teach us about our lives as Christians? (Compare I Cor. 12:12-27, especially vs. 26.)

_____

Following the central campaign directed against Jericho and Ai, the Israelites assembled between Mount Ebal and Mount Gerizim for a convocation to hear the reading of the Law of Moses (Josh. 8:30-35).

Soon after this the kingdoms to the south prepared a united attack upon the people of God (chap. 9). But one of these groups used a unique approach. The Gibeonites tricked Israel into making a covenant with them. Before long these same Gibeonites brought Israel into war with the entire southern confederacy (chap. 10). A remarkable battle it was! A God-sent hailstorm on Israel's enemies greatly assisted the victory. What else did God do during this battle in answer to Joshua's believing prayer (10:12-15)?

_____

God's supernatural power, through Christ, is available to give us victory over sin and Satan. Paul declares: "Now to him who is able to do immeasurably more than all we ask or imagine, according to his power that is at work within us" (Eph. 3:20).

Israel routed the enemy in a smashing victory, thus gaining control of the whole area, from Gibeon down to Kadesh Barnea. Only such city-states as Gezer and Jerusalem were not conquered.

When Jabin, king of Hazor, heard about Israel's triumphs in the south, he organized the northern kingdoms against Israel (chap. 11). These kings were not rulers of vast territories, but were local rulers of their cities and the surrounding countryside. Finally, Joshua took the enemy's last stronghold in a surprise attack upon Hazor itself.

Unfortunately, Joshua failed to seize the coastline from the Philistines and the Phoenicians, as well as other areas. This failure to fully take possession of the territory allotted to Israel sowed the seeds of all their future troubles. Even though Israel did not destroy all the inhabitants of Canaan, Joshua was able to divide the land as God had instructed him.

Divide

To DIVIDE the land was Joshua's next major task,

covered in the second half of the Book of Joshua (13—24).

Referring to a map in the back of your Bible, write on the map below the names of the 12 tribes to indicate the divisions of the land.

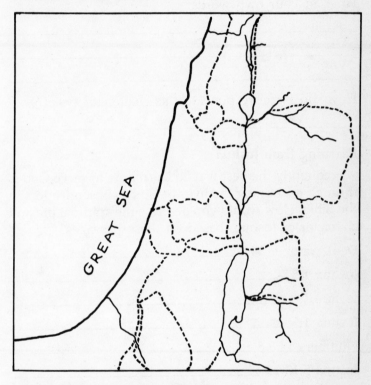

Since the men of the tribe of Levi were specially set apart for the service of the sanctuary, they were not apportioned territory as were the other eleven tribes, but were given 48 cities with pasture lands among all the tribes (Num. 35:1-8; Josh. 21:1-3).

Two and one half tribes were given their allotment on the east side of the Jordan. A major conflict arose when they erected a separate altar by the Jordan, to be nearer their own territory. This presumptuous act was first contested and then terminated by the western tribes. God's way was to have all the tribes gather three times yearly around the altar at Shiloh (Ex. 23:17). After the land was conquered and divided, Joshua, now 110 years old, gathered the nation together at Shechem to rehearse the history of Israel and to challenge the people. From Joshua 24:14, 15 summarize his charge to Israel in your own words.

_____

_____

_____

How did Israel respond to this challenge? (vs. 16)

_____

Learning from Joshua

Frequently the best way to learn how to serve God is through examining the lives of God's chosen leaders in the Bible. How would you describe the spiritual life and character of Joshua, based on these passages?

Deuteronomy 34:9 _____

Joshua 1:5 _____

Joshua 1:6 _____

Joshua 1:7 _____

Numbers 14:6-8 _____

Joshua 5:13-15 _____

Joshua 11:15 _____

Joshua 24:15 _____

Symbol for Period Four

Take a moment to review the basic symbol found at the beginning of this chapter. Then, memorize the added items (on the symbol at the left) that will enable you to recall the four key topics that we learned for this period.

J —————— ; J —————— C —————— ;
C —————— & D —————— .

The first letter, "J," appears before the rectangle—as "M" for Moses did before—and represents Moses' successor, JOSHUA. Only one arrow appears in the "jet stream" of the "landing rocket." It represents the JORDAN CROSSING, similar to the Red Sea Crossing in the Exodus symbol. Inside the rectangle is "C o D." As C.O.D. means "Collect on Delivery" for a package that arrives in the mail, here it represents that which happened when Israel arrived in the Promised Land. The "C" stands for CONQUER.

Turn the small "o" into an "and" (&) sign. The "D" stands for DIVIDE.

Now review the preceding material and draw the symbol for period four from memory and identify the period, Bible location, and key topics.

Complete symbol	Period name: —————————
	Bible location: —————————
	Key words:
	—————————
	—————————
	—————————
	————————— & —————————

PERIOD FIVE:
JUDGES

This is the symbol for the fifth period in Bible history, named JUDGES. The period of the Judges was the "Dark Ages" of Israel's history. In seven apostasies Israel forsook the Lord and turned to idolatry, and suffered the terrible consequences of her sin.

Following Joshua's death, the tribes continued to occupy additional Canaanite territories. What did Israel fail to do with the Canaanites? (Jdg. 1:19, 21, 25, 27-33)

During the period of the Judges, Israel had the opportunity to show its gratitude to God and its willingness to meet its covenant obligations. God had placed Israel in the land and had promised to be with her. This was a period of probation. But Israel failed again and again. What did God warn Israel would happen because of her incomplete obedience? (Jdg. 2:1-3)

Because Israel disobeyed God, she was repeatedly plundered and dominated by the very nations she was supposed to have conquered. It was then that God "raised up judges, who saved them" (Jdg. 2:16). The

Hebrew word for judge means one who dispenses justice, punishing the evildoer and vindicating the righteous. The judges were not the same as our modern conception of "judge." Normally they did not hold court or make legal decisions. These deliverers and temporary rulers did not inherit their authority, they were not kings. Moreover, their rule was territorial, not nationwide. Their periods of office, therefore, may have overlapped.

Judges

The history of the judges is covered in the Book of JUDGES. Thirteen judges are named: Othniel, Ehud, Shamgar, Deborah and Barak, Gideon, Tola, Jair, Jephthah, Ibzan, Elon, Abdon, and Samson. Underline the names of the judges beginning with the letters D, G, and S, in that order. These are the three judges that we especially want you to remember. Note that these three letters fit into the name juDGeS—which should further help you to remember them!

Two later judges, Eli and Samuel, are recorded in I Samuel. Samuel is the link between the judges and the kings of Israel.

The Book of Judges underlines the fact that God delights in using the weak or unusual things: left-handed assassin Ehud; Deborah, a woman; Gideon, an unknown from the smallest tribe; Shamgar and his ox goad; Gideon's small pitcher-armed band; and the jawbone used by Samson.

In our day too, God continues to use the weak things of this world to accomplish His purposes. For your encouragement, meditate on I Corinthians 1:26-31. What is God's overriding purpose in using weak things? (vs. 29; compare II Cor. 4:7)

Seven Apostasies

During the 400-year period of the judges, Israel experienced SEVEN APOSTASIES, each resulting in servitude to an enemy people. Israel's pattern is seen in the first cycle, as follows:

1. What evil did Israel fall into? (Jdg. 2:11-13)

_____

2. What judgment did God bring upon the nation of Israel? (Jdg. 2:14, 15)

_____

3. What did God do on Israel's behalf? (Jdg. 2:16)

_____

4. What moved God to look on Israel in mercy? (Jdg. 2:18)

_____

This fourfold cycle may be characterized by four words: sin, suffering, supplication, and salvation. It has somewhat cynically been said that the only thing we learn from history is that we do not learn from history. Check Judges 2:19-23 to see whether this was true of Israel.

_____

Sin

The cycle each time began with Israel's fall into SIN. Her association with the pagan people led her into apostasy, which usually involved idolatry.

Suffering

Because of her sin, Israel was judged by the Lord and became a SUFFERING people. Israel's oppressors and God's scourge among His people were the nations of Mesopotamia, Moab, Philistia, Canaan, Midian, Ammon, and Amalek. The boundaries of Israel disappeared during this period as the land was contested by the resurgent Canaanite tribes.

Supplication

In her sorrow, Israel eventually would repent and turn back to God with SUPPLICATION for deliverance from her oppressors.

Salvation

God raised up judges, or leaders, as His instruments to bring SALVATION to Israel. The names of the three outstanding judges whose names begin with the letters capitalized in the word juDGeS are: _____ , _____ and _____ . Let's take a closer look at each of these judges.

Deborah

DEBORAH and Barak served in the north during the third apostasy and rallied the tribesmen to a victorious battle against a Canaanite coalition formed in an attempt to crush the Hebrews.

For how many years had the Israelites been oppressed? (Jdg. 4:1-3)

_____

What pieces of evidence are there that Deborah was God's leader for this time? (Jdg. 4:4-9)

_____

Who killed the captain of Canaan's army, and how? (4:16-24)

_____

The story of Deborah shows us that God uses both men and women in giving victories to His people.

Gideon

GIDEON, perhaps the best known of these heroes, served in central Palestine during the fifth apostasy and defeated the devastating forays of Midian. Israel's oppression is described in Judges 6:1-6.

In what ways did God encourage Gideon to serve as His leader? (Jdg. 6:12-22)

How can these encouragements help you in your walk and service for God? (compare also Phil. 4:13 and II Cor. 12:7-9)

God gave Gideon two signs (Jdg. 6:17-21 and 6:36-40) as further assurance of His leading. He then directed Gideon to narrow down his forces from 32,000 to 300, as recorded in 7:2-8. Why did God do this?

Briefly describe the very unusual manner in which the Midianites were routed out of their camp? (Jdg. 7:15-23)

Gideon's humble refusal of kingship (Jdg. 8:23) was laudable, yet what sin did he then fall into? (Jdg. 8:24-27)

What message does this convey to us when we are used in God's service? (compare I Cor. 1:31; 10:12)

Samson

SAMSON, a popular hero of prodigious strength, fought Philistia during the seventh apostasy. His story is filled with opportunity and failure. Appointed by God before birth, Samson had everything in his favor; yet he engaged in disobedience and immorality that resulted in his downfall.

Samson was a "Nazirite," that is, a person who separated himself from others and consecrated himself to God in a special vow. What were the major prohibitions of the Nazirite vow? (Num. 6:2-8)

_____

Which of these did Samson disobey in Judges 14:8, 9?

_____

In what other way did Samson sin? (Jdg. 16:1, 4)

_____

Describe how Samson was led into violation of another of these prohibitions, which led to his downfall? (Jdg. 16:4-21)

_____

_____

Samson's grim sense of humor and headstrong reaction is seen in the ways that he got even with the Philistines, whom he intensely hated. To get the clothes reward for the Philistines who secured the answer to his riddle he (Jdg. 14:19):

_____

To take vengeance on his father-in-law who gave Samson's bride to another man he (Jdg. 15:3-6):

_____

_____

To avenge his bride's death he (Jdg. 15:7, 8):

_____

To retaliate when captured he (Jdg. 15:14-16):

_____

To retaliate when made fun of at the Philistine feast to their god Dagon he (Jdg. 16:26-30):

_____

Ruth

The Book of Ruth also finds its setting during the period of the judges, adding a bright picture to an otherwise dismal period. Ruth is the story of a woman from the idolatrous nation of Moab who chose to serve the God of Israel. The Book of Ruth demonstrates that God had a believing remnant in the land even in the dark, apostate days. It is a lesson in godly consistency.

Boaz's marriage to Ruth demonstrates the carrying out of the law of the kinsman redeemer (see Deut. 25:5-10). This law ruled that if a man died, his brother or the next nearest of kin must marry his widow to raise up children in his name. Boaz, second behind a brother who refused to marry Ruth, accepted Ruth and married her. Ruth, a foreigner to Israel, became the grandmother of David, and was placed in the ancestry of the Messiah. Boaz was the son of Rahab, the harlot of Jericho. Both Rahab and Ruth are listed in the bloodline of the Messiah (Mt. 1:5).

Learning About Biblical Purity

As you complete this study in the period of the Judges, you may be reminded of the Christian's constant temptation to compromise his or her witness to God in the world. We are *in* the world in order to be spiritual lights, but we must not be *of* the world, living with a polluted testimony. II Corinthians 6:17, 18 expresses a very important truth about the Christian walk: "Therefore come out from them and be separate, says the Lord. Touch no unclean thing, and I will receive you. I will be a Father to you, and you will be my sons and daughters, says the Lord Almighty."

In your own words, state how I Corinthians 10:13 applies to your life in relation to temptation and sin:

_____

_____

Symbol for Period Five

Take a moment to review the basic symbol found at the beginning of this chapter. Then, memorize the added items (on the symbol at the left) that will enable you to recall the key words of this period. Try to recall the words these items represent. Try not to look back in the lesson.

7 _____   S _____   S _____   S _____
S _____   D _____   G _____   S _____

The number 7 represents the **7 APOSTASIES** in which Israel went through the persistent cycle of **SIN**, **SUFFERING**, **SUPPLICATION**, and **SALVATION** (represented by the circle with four S's). The broken rectangle represents the uncertain boundaries of Israel during this period. The three letters underneath the rectangle represent three outstanding judges: **DEBORAH**, **GIDEON**, and **SAMSON**. Remember that these letters are the last three consonants of the word juDGeS.

Now, cover up the above material. Draw the complete symbol from memory, and fill in the blanks.

Complete symbol	Period name: _____
	Bible location: _____
	Key words:
	_____
	_____
	_____
	_____
	_____
	_____
	_____

6

PERIOD SIX:
UNITED KINGDOM

The symbol for period six shows a crown over a rectangle and represents the **UNITED KINGDOM**. As you learned, period five was a bleak time in Israel's history. By contrast, period six was one of the nation's brightest times. However there were lapses into sin even in this period, which covered the reigns of three Kings, each of which lasted 40 years.

I and II Samuel and I Kings 1—11

The establishment and glory of the Hebrew kingdom is presented in the Books of **I AND II SAMUEL** and **I KINGS 1—11**. I and II Chronicles covers this same ground from a later viewpoint in Jewish history.

Samuel: Organization

SAMUEL was the last of the judges and the first of the writing prophets. He was the person God used for the **ORGANIZATION** of the kingdom. By far the greatest of all the judges, he was called by God to anoint the first two kings of Israel.

When Samuel began his ministry, Israel was hard pressed to maintain any semblance of freedom as a nation. The Philistines had struck so often that the people lived in constant fear. If ever a nation needed a man of godliness and spiritual stature, Israel needed one when Samuel came upon the scene.

The declining office of judge, combined with corrupt and selfish priestly practices, was in worse shape than ever. Eli, the current priest, was a very indulgent and weak spiritual leader. He failed even to control his own sons, who made lust and selfish gratification their objectives in the Temple service. As a result, the populace abhorred the annual festivals. Spiritual interest waned and the people turned to other pursuits.

Samuel came on the scene like a refreshing rain on parched land. Born of godly parents, he was first presented to the Lord, then allowed to stay at the Tabernacle to assist in the divine services (I Sam. 1:21-28). While he was yet a child, God called Samuel to serve Him (chap. 3). Following Eli's death, Samuel became priest at Shiloh. He also was established in Israel as a prophet and a judge (3:20, 21; 7:15-17).

Given in answer to the prayers of his devout mother Hannah, (I Samuel 1) Samuel was himself a man of the Word and of prayer. His ministry to Israel may be summarized in I Samuel 12:23: "As for me, far be it from me that I should sin against the Lord by failing to pray for you. And I will teach you the way that is good and right."

Saul: Evil Heart

The first king of Israel was SAUL (I Samuel 9—31). Samuel was greatly distressed when the nation demanded a king to rule over them. What were two reasons Israel gave for wanting a king? (I Sam. 8:4, 5, 20)

_____

_____

What was wrong with Israel's motive for wanting a king? (I Sam. 8:6, 7)

_____

What warning did Samuel give Israel about their request for a king? (I Sam. 8:9-18)

_____

What was it about Saul that may have attracted Israel to him? (I Samuel 9:1, 2)

_____

Saul began well and, for a while, was obedient to the will of God. But he later became self-willed, abusive, and controlled by pride.

Israel was controlled by the Philistines when Saul began his reign. It was Saul's noble son Jonathan who destroyed the Philistine garrison, broke through their companies, and reestablished contact between Benjamin and the northern tribes.

Despite Jonathan's victories, Saul's glory was short-lived. He later degenerated into a savage and jealous tyrant. He failed as a king, and ultimately perished in battle. Overall, Saul had an EVIL HEART.

David: Good Heart

Saul was succeeded by DAVID around 1000 B.C. (I Sam. 16—31 and II Sam.). He was the best king that Israel ever had. David's early career is interwoven with the life of King Saul, beginning with the defeat of the giant Goliath (I Sam. 17). What were the people saying about David that changed Saul's attitude toward him? (18:7-9)

_____

Filled with envy, Saul pursued David in a cat and mouse chase for ten years. First David remained near his headquarters at Gibeah, while Saul attempted to destroy him. Later David fled to the southern wilderness of Judea and moved back and forth between the Dead Sea and Philistia (I Samuel 20—30).

Following Saul's death in battle (chap. 31), David became king. For seven and a half years, his kingdom was confined to the south, with his capital in Hebron; while Saul's son Ishbosheth ruled over Gilead in his capital of Mahanaim (II Sam. 2:8-11).

When Ishbosheth was murdered by his angered general, David became king over all Israel (II Sam. 5:4, 5). He captured the stronghold of Jerusalem from the Jebusites and made it his religious and political capital (II Sam. 5:6-10). He succeeded in bringing the Ark of the Covenant to the new city of "Zion" and made worship central in the nation's life. He also gained a decisive victory over the long-term enemy Philistia; organized Israel's government; and extended her territories up toward the Euphrates River on the northeast and to the Nile River on the southwest.

David had a **GOOD HEART**. Centuries later the apostle Paul declared that God saw in David "a man after my own heart" (Acts 13:22). David was a man sensitive to the Spirit of God; a man of deep faith, great courage, and a dependent heart. In spite of his manifest weaknesses and sins, David had a desire for God's presence in his life.

David made the greatest contribution of any king before or after him toward establishment of God's rule in the nation. David's rule became the standard by which all later kings were judged.

As with all men however, David was not perfect. What was David's grievous sin? (II Sam. 11) Describe its results.

_____

_____

Nathan the prophet, using a touching parable, pictured David's sin under the guise of someone else's imagined crime (II Sam. 12). When David raged against this imagined criminal, Nathan turned on the king and declared, "You are the man!" This rebuke went straight to David's heart. His conscience was smitten. The cries of David's repentance are preserved in Psalms 32 and

51. While God forgave David when he repented, he still reaped the fruit of his sins. What was Nathan's terrible declaration? (II Sam. 12:10)

_____

_____

Perilous years followed David's sin of seducing Bathsheba and arranging for the death of Uriah. Note the catalog of domestic troubles recorded in I Sam. 12—14. For a while David was even driven into exile by his own son Absalom (II Samuel 15—33).

Solomon: Divided Heart

David was succeeded by his son SOLOMON, whose history is recorded in I Kings 1—11. Solomon reigned in a golden era of peace and prosperity, and gained international recognition. Read Solomon's dream in II Kings 3:5-14. What attitude did Solomon express?

_____

What request did he make?

_____

What else did God promise him?

_____

What condition was attached to a prolonged life of God's blessing?

_____

Solomon saw this God-given dream fulfilled during his life. He was given great wisdom, which he used to lead the nation in a long period of peace and prosperity. More wealth came to Solomon however, than to the people. Taxation became an oppressive burden for the people during Solomon's reign.

In spite of his greatness, Solomon often failed to please God because he had a DIVIDED HEART. Read I Kings 11:1-8, where events near the end of Solomon's life are described. What was the root cause of his turning away from the Lord?

Poetical Books

The **POETICAL BOOKS** (Job, Psalms, Proverbs, Ecclesiastes and Song of Solomon) fit into this period of Israel's history. Psalms, the "Hebrew Prayer and Praise Book," is the heart of the Bible. David is credited with 73 of the Psalms. Proverbs is a guidebook for successful living. Ecclesiastes emphasizes the vanity of life apart from the will of God. The Song of Solomon speaks of the beauty of physical love between a man and a woman. Some see it as symbolic of Christ's love for the Church. Job speaks to the age-old question of why the righteous suffer.

Temple

Solomon's chief accomplishment was the building of the **TEMPLE**, which had been planned by David. Erected during the first decade of Solomon's reign, the Temple represents a high point in Israel's religious history. Built on the top of Mount Moriah, where Abraham had many years before gone to sacrifice Isaac, Solomon's Temple was never equaled in beauty. When it was completed, Solomon addressed the people and led them in a prayer of dedication (I Ki. 8:22-61). As the Psalms gave expression to Israel's worship of God, the Temple provided a central place for Israel's worship.

Learning About Leadership

Even though Eli was God's priest at the Temple, God held him responsible (I Sam. 3:13) for the wicked living of his sons (I Sam. 2:12, 17, 22). What principle does this teach us about our ministry at home? (compare I Tim. 3:4)

Samuel was called by God to proclaim His words to Israel. In what two major areas is Samuel's ministry an example we should seek to follow? (Check out I Sam. 3:19-21 and 12:23 as you prepare your answer.)

_____

_____

On the other hand, Saul provides a number of negative lessons about leadership. For example, Saul took credit when Jonathan smote the Philistines (I Sam. 13:3, 4). Also, Saul failed to wait on God, but instead took matters into his own hands (I Sam. 13:8-15).

Saul's leadership was marked by undue severity (I Sam. 14:24; 43, 44), and he was eventually turned away from following God by his desire for personal gain (I Sam. 15:9). Failing to accept personal responsibility for his actions, he blamed others (I Sam. 15:15, 17) and became a fearful follower of people, rather than a real leader (I Sam. 15:24). How does Proverbs 29:25 speak to this issue?

_____

King David provides us with many good examples of leadership. Note for each of the following passages the characteristic that marked David as a great leader.

I Samuel 17:45-47 _____

I Sam. 18:18; II Sam. 7:18 _____

I Sam. 23:2, 4, 9-12; II Sam. 2:1 _____

I Sam. 26:8-11 _____

II Sam. 9:1-13 _____

Symbol for Period Six

Take a moment to review the basic symbol found at the beginning of this chapter. Then, memorize the added items (on the symbol at the left) that

54

will enable you to recall the key words of this period. Can you name the key words?

S _____ — O _____ ;
S _____ — E _____ ;
D _____ — G _____ ;
S _____ — D _____ ;
P _____   B _____ ;
T _____ .

The first represents **SAMUEL**, whom God used for the **ORGANIZATION** of the kingdom (represented by the big O that appears to embrace the rectangle). Three letters inside the rectangle represent the three kings. **SAUL** is the first—the darkened heart represents his **EVIL HEART**. David is next—the white heart represents his **GOOD HEART**. Last is Solomon—the half-and-half heart represents his **DIVIDED HEART**. The musical lyre underneath David's heart represents the **POETICAL BOOKS**. The last drawing is Solomon's **TEMPLE**.

Now cover up the preceding material and draw the complete symbol for period six from memory and identify the period, location, and key words.

Complete symbol	Period name: _____
	Bible location: _____
	Key words:
	_____ — _____
	_____ — _____
	_____ — _____
	_____ — _____
	_____ _____
	_____

7

PERIOD SEVEN:
DIVIDED KINGDOM

This is the symbol for period seven. The United Kingdom now becomes the **DIVIDED KINGDOM**. In this period the kingdom was torn into two parts.
Rehoboam (931 B.C.), Solomon's son, continued his father's high taxation. The ten northern tribes under the leadership of Jeroboam revolted and set up an independent kingdom, Israel, which he ruled from Samaria. The two remaining tribes became the kingdom of Judah (named after its prominent tribe), and remained loyal to the Davidic throne. Each nation had its own succession of kings.

I Kings 12—II Kings

The story of the Divided Kingdom is told in **I KINGS 12—II KINGS**. These chapters record the decline and fall of both Israel and Judah. They also provide the historical setting for the Old Testament books of prophecy.

Kings of Israel: All Bad

The **KINGS OF ISRAEL** were Jeroboam, Nadab, Baasha, Elah, Zimri, Omri and Tibni, Ahab, Ahaziah, Jehoram, Jehu, Jehoahaz, Joash, Jeroboam II, Zachariah, Shallum, Menahem, Pekahiah, Pekah, and Hoshea.

The nineteen kings of Israel were **ALL BAD**. Not a single one paid heed to the true worship of God. The pagan calf worship instituted by Jeroboam remained a constant snare to the northern tribes.

Ahab and Elijah

The most infamous of Israel's kings was **AHAB**. Turn to I Kings 16:29-33 to read a description of Ahab. In what three key areas did Ahab's wickedness abound? (vs. 31) (Compare Deut. 7:1-4 and Ex. 20:4.)

_____

_____

Ahab married Jezebel, daughter of Tyre's priest-king, in order to ratify an alliance between Tyre and Israel. Provision was made for her to continue worshiping her native god Baal in Samaria (I Ki. 16:31-33). Jezebel clamored for the propagation of the Baal cult and the extermination of those who worshiped Jehovah (I Ki. 18:4, 13). This activity brought her into direct conflict with the prophet Elijah.

Elijah was a striking character with long hair who wore a sheepskin cloak. He thundered out warnings to idolatrous Israel during Ahab's reign. Many of the episodes of his life involved a clash between the worship of Jehovah and Baal. Perhaps the most awesome incident was the contest at Mt. Carmel, where God spectacularly demonstrated His superiority over Baal (I Kings 18).

Elijah had predicted that God would judge both Ahab and Jezebel. In a war with Syria, Ahab was mortally wounded by a random arrow (I Ki. 22). Soon afterward Jezebel came to her grisly end (II Ki. 9:30-37).

Elijah was succeeded by Elisha, whose ministry spanned more than 50 years (II Ki. 2-9). Most of his miracles were deeds of kindness and mercy.

Kings of Judah: Eight Good

The **KINGS OF JUDAH** were Rehoboam, Abijah, Asa,

Jehoshaphat, Jehoram, Ahaziah, Athaliah, Joash, Amaziah, Azariah, Jotham, Ahaz, Hezekiah, Manasseh, Amon, Josiah, Jehoahaz, Jehoiakim, Jehoiachin, Zedekiah (I Ki. 15:1-24; II Ki. 12—23; II Chron. 10—36). There were **EIGHT GOOD** kings among Judah's twenty. They were: Asa, Jehoshaphat, Joash, Amaziah, Azariah (Uzziah), Jotham, Hezekiah, and Josiah.

Hezekiah

One of the outstanding good kings of Judah was **HEZEKIAH**. He was used of God to bring a great revival to the nation. At the very outset of his reign he sought spiritual and political reformation. True worship was reestablished, and the covenant with Jehovah was reaffirmed. The Temple was reopened and all signs of idolatry were rooted out (II Ki. 18—20; II Chron. 29—32; Isa. 36—39).

How does II Chronicles 31:20, 21 summarize Hezekiah's leadership?

_____

_____

However, God allowed Sennacherib, king of Assyria, to come against Judah. How did Hezekiah respond to this invasion threat? (II Chron. 32:2-5)

_____

_____

How did he encourage the people in II Chronicles 32:6-8?

_____

The mature spirituality of Hezekiah's life is further seen in his response to Sennacherib's demand for submission. What was that response? (Isa. 37:14-20)

_____

Isaiah came as God's messenger to Hezekiah (Isa.

37:21). How did this invasion threat end? (Isa. 37:36, 37)

Later, when Hezekiah became fatally ill, God answered his prayer with the promise to add fifteen years to his life and to defend him from Assyria.

Josiah

Hezekiah's reign was followed by 57 years of apostasy under his son Manasseh and grandson Amon. Then his great-grandson JOSIAH ascended the throne at eight years of age. He reigned 31 years (II Ki. 22, 23; II Chron. 34—35). How is Josiah's reign summarized in II Chronicles 34:2?

Josiah served at one of the most fateful turning points in Judah's history. He was the last of the good kings. He brought the nation back to God. At the young age of 16 he began seeking after God. He took firm measures against wickedness and pagan worship.

Josiah repaired the Temple that had fallen into total neglect. While the Temple was being repaired and cleaned, a scroll was found that proved to be a copy of the "Book of the Covenant" of the Lord. Its discovery brought a great stir. Josiah called an assembly and read the scroll.

What did he do after this reading? (II Chron. 34:29-32)

What else did the king do? (II Chron. 34:33)

Prophets

At this critical period in the nation's history God called forth His PROPHETS—to warn of evil and injustice, and to inspire righteousness. They spoke primarily by means of warnings and gave encouragement concerning the future. They prophesied the fall of the nation, and led the people to look for the glory of Israel through the coming Messiah.

Most of the prophets ministered and wrote before the Babylonian Captivity, including Isaiah, Jeremiah, and eight of the minor prophets.

Two of these prophets, Amos and Hosea, ministered to the northern kingdom of Israel, before the nation was taken into captivity.

AMOS presented a series of judgments ("burdens" in some translations) upon the nations and upon Israel and Judah, revealing God's inevitable judgment on sin. He concluded with the promise of the Messiah who would bless a restored Israel.

HOSEA pronounced doom upon the ten tribes of Israel for their unfaithfulness. Yet he also pointed the way of deliverance for Israel through God's compassion—as illustrated in his own marriage.

Six prophets ministered to the southern kingdom of Judah before her captivity.

JOEL interpreted a locust plague as foreshadowing future judgment in the "Day of the Lord." He prophesied the outpouring of the Spirit upon all flesh to unite all as one in the Messiah.

ISAIAH, truly the greatest of the Old Testament prophets, pronounced judgment and then outlined the great Messianic plan of God in the atoning work of the Lord's Servant, and the glorious reign of the Prince of Peace.

MICAH prophesied against Israel's and Judah's sins. He pronounced the nation lost, but declared it would ultimately be restored and the Messianic kingdom would be established.

ZEPHANIAH predicted desolation because of Judah's rebellion and idolatry. He predicted her restoration and the extension of God's salvation to the nations after the judgment.

JEREMIAH scorned apostate Judah for her vices, crimes, and idolatries, and called her to repentance. He predicted her sure doom and urged her to surrender to Nebuchadnezzar.

HABAKKUK prophesied doom for Israel and for the Chaldean Kingdom, that sinful nation which God later used to punish Israel. He called men and women to live by faith.

Two prophets spoke to the Assyrian kingdom of Nineveh during this era.

JONAH called Nineveh to repentance and revival resulted. God's love and plan for the Gentiles was revealed.

NAHUM, about 150 years after Jonah, pronounced the impending destruction of Nineveh.

A prevalent aspect in the prophets' message concerns the promised Messiah. Messianic prophecy presents revelations of the Person of the Messiah—His nature, character, life, experiences, and performance. A second major idea presented in Messianic prophecy is the kingdom as a perfect rule of righteousness and justice on the earth.

Learning to Serve

We can often better learn how to serve by evaluating the way people in the Bible have served. In some cases we may learn things to avoid. Certainly the lives of many of the kings of Israel teach us that! In other cases we can learn things that will help us serve God better. What qualities of spiritual leadership, practiced by Elijah in the following passages, are also important in your service for God?

I Kings 17:1-5; 18:1, 2

I Kings 17:7-16 (Compare Ps. 37:25 or Phil. 4:19.)

I Kings 18:24, 36, 37, 41-45

I Kings 21:17-24

Symbol for Period Seven

Take a moment to review the basic symbol found at the beginning of this chapter. Then, memorize the added items (on the symbol at the left) that will enable you to recall the key words of this period. Write the key words below.

I _____ = A _____

A _____

J _____ = E _____

H _____ , J _____

P _____

The first part of the broken crown, now marked "I," represents KINGS OF ISRAEL. The sad face on a zero represents ALL BAD. One example, AHAB, is represented by the "A." It may help you to relate "all bad" and "Ahab." The second part of the broken crown, now marked "J," represents KINGS OF JUDAH. The happy face on a figure "8" represents EIGHT GOOD kings. Two examples, HEZEKIAH and JOSIAH are represented by the letters "H" and "J." Note that both end in "iah." Relating the two "J's" will aid in remembering. The open-mouthed circle underneath the rectangle represents the PROPHETS.

Now cover up the page above this line and draw the complete symbol. Also write the name of the period, the Bible reference, and each of the key words.

Complete symbol	Period name: _____
	Bible location: _____

Key words:

_____ = _____

_____

_____ = _____

_____ , _____

_____

8

PERIOD EIGHT:
CAPTIVITY

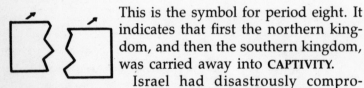
This is the symbol for period eight. It indicates that first the northern kingdom, and then the southern kingdom, was carried away into CAPTIVITY.

Israel had disastrously compromised truth and faith in idolatrous worship. This led to a virtual abandonment of her worship of the Lord. First Israel, and later Judah, were carried away by foreign powers. Israel was never heard of again, and Judah spent 70 punitive years in captivity. God used these years, however, as Judah learned once and for all not to bow before pagan idols.

II Kings

In II Kings we read of the captivities: of Israel in chapter 17; and of Judah in chapters 24 and 25. II Chronicles 36:5-21 and Jeremiah 39 and 52 also deal with the captivities.

The prophets who ministered to Judah during the captivity were Jeremiah, Ezekiel, and Daniel. Obadiah wrote against the nation of Edom, descendants of Jacob's brother Esau.

Israel: Assyria, Scattered

For 130 years the northern kingdom of ISRAEL had lived under the threat of Assyrian attack. Serious internal instability gripped the nation during these years. The majority of their last kings were victims of assassination. The prophet Hosea refers to this relentless pattern of intrigue (Hos. 7:7). Israel's resources were seriously depleted by decades of warring or paying tribute to avoid battle. She scarcely survived the attacks of the mighty king Tiglath Pileser, who carved off huge portions from her boundaries.

Finally, during Hoshea's rule, Israel was destroyed by ASSYRIA, as Shalmaneser V swept into Israel. Following the capture of Israel's other cities, Shalmaneser's armies surrounded the capital city of Samaria. The fortress held out for two years. Then a new king, Sargon II, finished the task in 722 B.C. God had used a pagan nation, Assyria, to bring judgment on His idolatrous people.

The Assyrian kings then SCATTERED the ten tribes to eastern parts of their empire. Some 27,000 people of the upper classes were deported. The policy of deportation was a means of discouraging revolt. Natural leaders were less likely to start a rebellion if they were transplanted to distant parts and settled among aliens. Few people, if any, ever returned from the Assyrian captivity. Israel thus gradually disappeared, becoming the "lost tribes" of history.

The capital of Samaria was desolated, just as had been predicted in Amos 5:2, 3. The area was then repopulated by settlers that the Assyrians brought from other parts of the empire (II Ki. 17:24). These foreigners intermarried with the Israelites who had been left behind. In time the whole of Palestine, except the little kingdom of Judea, became populated by these peoples of mixed heritage.

These same foreign peoples introduced their own pagan religions into the land. Later, however, they found it expedient to worship the Lord as well. Why was this so? (II Ki. 17:25-28)

This mixed population, with its mixed religion (II Ki. 17:29-33) became the Samaritan race of the New Testament period.

Judah: Babylonia, Exiled

The southern kingdom of JUDAH fell approximately 150 years later than Israel. Though Hezekiah had resisted collaboration with Assyria, his son Manasseh was bent the opposite way. His political submission was accompanied by a reversion to pagan practices of idolatry and astrology.

From II Kings 21:1-9, 16, summarize the Biblical assessment of Manasseh's reign.

_____

_____

The trend set by Manasseh now moved relentlessly to disaster. Even Josiah's revival could not measurably alter the consequences of Judah's forsaking the Lord God. Josiah's successors ruled on terms set by the Egyptian or Babylonian kings. Just as predicted by the prophets, disobedience to God's Law brought judgment.

Assyria attempted to capture Judah, but was turned away when Hezekiah earnestly sought the Lord (II Ki. 18:13—19:37). During the closing years of Judah's history, Babylonia replaced Assyria as a world power.

Judah was finally conquered by BABYLONIA under King Nebuchadnezzar. In three separate campaigns, from 605 B.C. to 586 B.C., he systematically destroyed the cities of Judah, deporting most of the Jewish people, and exiling them to colonies in Babylon. In various excavations of Judah's cities, absolute destruction is apparent. Judah's defeat was made more painful because Syria, Moab, and Ammon, neighboring nations, aided Nebuchadnezzar in destroying Judah.

King Zedekiah, the last king of Judah, was encouraged to rebel against Babylon. Nebuchadnezzar responded by laying siege to the city, slowly starving the people into submission. Finally in 586 B.C., after eighteen months of siege, Nebuchadnezzar again captured the capital. This time there was no mercy at all. The city walls were torn down and the Temple and houses of the king were burned. This tragic tale is related in II Kings 25.

From II Chronicles 36:14-16, what were two key reasons for the destruction and captivity of Judah?

_____

_____

After executing a number of the principal religious and civil leaders, over 20,000 people of the upper and middle classes were EXILED to Babylonia. Jeremiah's numbers (Jer. 52:28-30) probably include only the important families. New settlers were brought in from surrounding nations to repopulate the desolated areas. The land was, at last, to enjoy its Sabbath rest (II Chron. 36:21).

Effects of the Exile

In punishing God's disobedient people, the captivity of Judah had two important results:

MONOTHEISM (THE BELIEF IN ONE GOD) WAS FULLY EMBRACED. The Exile resulted in the extinction of idolatry among the Jews. Their captivity brought to the people a keen realization of their sin and its punishment, and of the true nature of the Lord. In Babylon they saw idolatry at its worst. Though some abandoned their faith and lusted after the goddesses of Babylon, the remnant heeded the warnings of God's prophets, realizing that the Exile was God's punishment for their idolatry. When the people returned from captivity they were a transformed people. Never again would idols be openly tolerated by God's chosen people.

A DISPERSION OF GOD'S PEOPLE WAS ACCOMPLISHED.

God's covenant with Abraham was: "all peoples on earth will be blessed through you." Now God dispersed His people throughout the world—to areas that became Persia, Greece, Egypt, Syria, and Rome. In all these places the Jews blessed their pagan neighbors. How did Micah express this in his prophecy? (Mic. 5:7)

_____

_____

The Jews' worship of the Lord, their honorable family life, and their study of the Law and the Prophets established an island of praise to the Lord in the midst of a sea of paganism. In their adversity, God fulfilled His promise.

The Judean community in Babylon had a rich religious heritage. They learned to retain the worship of God, even without the Temple or its sacrifices. During this time the synagogue arose as the meeting place of the Jews in a local community. From the people of the Judean dispersion would come those who would return to rebuild Jerusalem.

In the New Testament period the dispersed Jews provided many opportunities for Paul to proclaim Christ to both Jews and Gentiles.

Prophets in the Exile

The prophet Jeremiah, whose ministry began before the Exile, continued to serve God after the fall of Jerusalem. We are dependent almost exclusively on Jeremiah 39—45 for the events in Judah after the destruction of Jerusalem. Jeremiah's Lamentations expresses the anguish of the Jews over the ruin of their city, its Temple and its people.

How many years did Jeremiah prophesy that the Exile would last? (Jer. 25:11, 12)

_____

_____

Daniel laid claim to this promise about 50 years after the destruction of Jerusalem (Dan. 9:1, 2). God fulfilled His promise, and the Jews were allowed to return after the 70 years were completed. This story is told for us in the Books of Ezra and Nehemiah.

Both Daniel and Ezekiel were written during the Exile. Daniel was one of the youths taken in the first deportation to Babylon, where he was trained for service in the king's palace. There he became God's representative to the government of Babylon.

Daniel proclaimed that one day the kingdoms of this world would be replaced by the Kingdom of God. He traced the history of the Gentile powers from Babylon to the end. Daniel drew back the curtain and revealed the hidden things of the future as no one had ever done before. He is quoted most in Revelation, and knowledge of his prophecies is essential to understand this last book of the Bible.

Ezekiel was taken to Babylon in the second deportation. While Daniel served in the palace, Ezekiel was perhaps toiling in a slave gang. His primary task was to proclaim God's truth to the exiled Jews and to explain the real meaning of their plight. He was God's spokesman and watchman. To those who remained true to the Lord, he was a counselor, herald of salvation, expositor of godliness, and the one who saw God's restoration of the nation and the universal reign of the Messiah.

One prophet, Obadiah, condemned Edom for its treachery toward Judah. Edom's utter destruction and Judah's salvation in the Day of the Lord is the subject of this shortest prophecy and smallest book of the Old Testament.

Learning Through Discipline

Scripture instructs us about God's purpose in discipline. We should note that there is a difference between discipline and punishment. Read Hebrews 12:1-13 in this regard. The Christians to whom this book was addressed were Jews, living in a time of great religious and political stress. The Jewish people were preparing a revolt against Rome and were pressuring every Jew to conform to their political and religious principles. Extreme pressure was exercised to stamp out their faith in Jesus the Messiah.

In order to help the wavering faith of these Christians, the writer first reminded them (in chap. 11) of the faith of many men and women of God who had lived during the Old Testament period. These believers are said to be "a great cloud of witnesses" (12:1) who are now examples to them in their struggles. Following this encouragement, the author lists three vital keys to victory. These are (Heb. 12:1-3):

1. _____

2. _____

3. _____

He then links their persecution and God's discipline, in Hebrews 12:4-16. How were these Christians to view their persecution? (vss. 4-6)

_____

What is God's purpose in discipline? (vss. 7-10)

_____

What attitude is needed in order for discipline to be effective? (vss. 11-13)

_____

Symbol for Period Eight

Take a moment to review the basic symbol found at the beginning of this chapter. Then, memorize the added items (on the symbol at the left) that will enable you to recall the key words of this period. Name the key words:

```
I _____ — A _____
S _____ ;
J _____ — B _____
E _____
```

The letters represent the following: ISRAEL was captured by ASSYRIA and was SCATTERED. JUDAH was captured by BABYLONIA and was EXILED. As a memory aid,
note the alphabetical order of I/J and A/B. The supporting letters, AS and BE are alphabetical as well.

Cover up the above material and draw the complete
symbol. Also write the name of the period, the Bible
location, and each of the key words:

Complete symbol	Period name: _____
	Bible location: _____
	Key words:
	_____ — _____
	_____ ;
	_____ — _____
	_____

9

PERIODS NINE AND TEN:
RESTORATION & SILENT YEARS

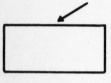 Following the Jews' 70 years captivity in Babylon, God reestablished a remnant of His people back in the city of Jerusalem. Period nine, the RESTORATION, is symbolized by the rectangle and the arrow pointing backward.

Ezra and Nehemiah

The history of these events in Jerusalem is presented in EZRA and NEHEMIAH. The Book of Esther sheds further light on God's preservation of His people in the dispersion.

The last three minor prophets, Haggai, Zechariah, and Malachi ministered to the Jews during the restoration.

Return from Persia

During the Exile, many Jews entered into commercial or agricultural pursuits in Babylon. There they prospered—and forgot their religion. But a remnant remained true to their faith and longed to see the time when they might be permitted to return to the land God had given their forefathers.

Following Nebuchadnezzar's death, civil wars erupted, resulting in the disintegration of the Babylonian empire. In 539 B.C. the empire fell to the united armies of the Medes and the Persians. Cyrus became the ruler of this great empire.

The new emperor won the gratitude of the exiles by reversing the deportation policy practiced by the Assyrian and Babylonian conquerors. In 538 B.C. he issued a decree that freed the Jews and permitted them to **RETURN FROM PERSIA** to Palestine. He even helped them rebuild their cities and places of worship.

What did God also call Cyrus to do? (Ezra 1:2-4)

Amazingly, Isaiah had named Cyrus 150 years before his reign, as the "shepherd" whom God would use to liberate His people from captivity (Isa. 44:28—45:4).

Most Jews had grown comfortable in Babylon and did not choose to leave. Only a relatively few enthusiasts and idealists accepted the king's permission to return to Jerusalem that first year. But many small groups did return in the following years, even though they experienced hardship, discouragement, and alternating failures and triumphs.

Zerubbabel: Temple

Close to 50,000 people were in the first group to return to Jerusalem (Ezra 2:64, 65). The active leaders of the people were **ZERUBBABEL**, a prince of the house of David; and Jeshua, the high priest.

Soon after they arrived in Jerusalem, Zerubbabel and Jeshua led the people in laying the foundation of the **TEMPLE**. The racially mixed people from Samaria expressed interest in the building program, but the zealous Jews denied them participation. The Samaritans then responded with hostility, slandering the Jews to the Persian king, successfully stopping the Temple reconstruction for about 15 years.

The Prophets After Exile

Early in the reign of Darius, God raised up Haggai.

What was the message of his prophecy? (Hag. 1:2-8)

_____

Why had the people not prospered in the land? (Hag. 1:5, 6-11)

_____

As a result of his urgent preaching, the work of rebuilding was resumed. Haggai's book is filled with encouragement to build. As a practical man of action, he worked alongside those who built.

When the work was again challenged by the Samaritans, Darius was encouraged to search for Cyrus's decree that first authorized the rebuilding. Upon its discovery, Darius commanded that the work be allowed to proceed. He also commanded his governors in neighboring provinces to supply materials (Ezra 5, 6).

Though the new structure was not as elaborate as Solomon's Temple had been, what did Haggai declare concerning it? (Hag. 2:9)

_____

After Haggai stirred the people to rebuild, Zechariah began his ministry of encouragement to the builders. Both prophets urged the rebuilding of the Temple as a necessary condition for God's renewed blessing upon Israel. How did Zechariah encourage the governor Zerubbabel in the difficult task of rebuilding the Temple? (Zech. 4:6-8)

_____

Zechariah also called Israel to a new mission to the nations. He envisioned for Israel the drawing of other peoples and nations to God through their witness in living (Zech. 8). Next to Isaiah, Zechariah is considered the most important Messianic prophet in the Old Testament. Chapters 9—14 contain abundant references to the coming Messiah.

Malachi, probably a contemporary of Ezra and Nehemiah, preached against the cynical, indifferent, and unscrupulous attitudes of the people. One by one, Malachi identified arguments that his people raised against God, and each time answered the argument. He emphasized pure hearts as well as works of righteousness. He viewed the Messiah's coming as a time of cleansing of the people's sins (Mal. 3:1-3).

Ezra: People

After the rebuilding of the Temple, God's people became complacent and the flame of faith once again burned low. Then, about a half-century after the Temple was completed, God raised up EZRA to lead a second expedition from Babylon to reinforce the struggling colonists in Palestine (Ezra 7—10). Over 1,700 men accompanied him. When Ezra arrived in Jerusalem and learned of the intermarriage of the Jews with the Canaanites, he responded in an agonizing prayer of confession on behalf of the people (Ezra 9:5-15).

How did the Jewish leaders respond to Ezra's prayer? (10:1-5)

_____

Ezra was a scribe, a student of the Law of Moses. He had a spiritual ministry to the PEOPLE of God. He called Israel back to the proper observance of Moses' law and led her in worship.

Ezra read the Law to the people as they were assembled for the Feast of Tabernacles (Neh. 8—10). There the people agreed to renew their covenant with God. Name at least six things the people agreed to do when they recommited themselves to God (Neh. 10:28-39).

_____   _____

_____   _____

_____   _____

75

Under Ezra there was a great revival of the study of Scripture.

Nehemiah: Walls

NEHEMIAH was a Jew who served as cupbearer in the Persian court of Artaxerxes I. While serving there, his relatives from Judea brought him news which caused him great remorse. What was this news? (Neh. 1:3, 4)

_____

Learning of Nehemiah's concern, the king commissioned him to return to Jerusalem to rebuild the WALLS and to serve as governor of Judah. Nehemiah returned to Jerusalem 14 years after Ezra had come there.

One night, after a secretive inspection of the city walls, Nehemiah called upon the people to aid him in rebuilding the ruined fortifications. With the loyal aid of the Jews, the walls were rebuilt in an amazingly short period of two months. This was in spite of fierce resistance from Sanballat the Samaritan, and other hostile neighbors.

Learning from Nehemiah's Leadership

Nehemiah was a spiritual administrator who knew how to lead God's people in the work of God. What prominent activity was an important key to his success? (Neh. 1:5-11; 2:4; 4:4, 5, 9; 6:9, 14; 13:14, 22, 29)

_____

What challenge do the following verses give as you seek answers to your prayers?

I John 3:22 _____

I John 5:14, 15 _____

Mark 11:24 _____

James 5:17, 18 _____

Luke 11:5-10 _____

76

Nehemiah is also an example of perseverance in our work for God. He faced many of the same types of opposition that you may experience. Record in the space below Nehemiah's method of handling this opposition.

Opposition: Displeasure (2:9, 10)

Nehemiah's response: (2:11-16) _____

_____

Opposition: Mockery (2:19)

Nehemiah's response: (2:20) _____

_____

Opposition: Ridicule (4:1-3)

Nehemiah's response: (4:4-6) _____

_____

Opposition: Anger (4:7, 8)

Nehemiah's response: (4:9) _____

_____

Opposition: Discouragement & Intimidation (4:1-12)

Nehemiah's response: (4:13-23) _____

_____

Opposition: Selfish greed (5:1-5)

Nehemiah's response: (5:6-19) _____

_____

Opposition: Intimidation (6:1-7)

Nehemiah's response: (6:8, 9) _____

_____

Opposition: Cunning deceit (6:10, 11)

Nehemiah's response: (6:12-16) _____

_____

Esther: Protection

The Jews who remained in Persia after the Captivity ended faced great danger. While God was at work in Jerusalem, Satan was masterminding a plot to obliterate the Jews remaining in Persia. The Book of ESTHER is the story of God's PROTECTION of these Jews. Although the name of God is not mentioned in this book, divine providence and care are apparent throughout. Here are the highlights of this dramatic story:

King Ahasuerus first ostracized his queen, and then selected Esther, a young Jewish orphan, to replace her. Meanwhile, Esther's cousin Mordecai uncovered an assassination plot against the king and reported it.

Unfortunately, Mordecai got into trouble for refusing to bow to the king's officials. Haman, one of them, was so incensed by this that he devised a grand plot to kill Mordecai, along with all the Jews in the empire. Mordecai's only hope was to prevail on Esther to intercede with the king on behalf of her people.

When the king learned that Mordecai had saved his life, Ahasuerus recruited Haman and made him honor Mordecai! When the king learned that Haman had plotted to kill all the Jews, he had Haman hanged on the high gallows which had been built for Mordecai.

Nevertheless, the decree to exterminate all the Jews had been issued. The law of the Medes and Persians could never be changed. How did the Jews escape annihilation? (Esth. 8:10-13; 9:1, 2)

PERIOD TEN: 400 SILENT YEARS

This simple symbol represents period ten, the SILENT YEARS. The Old Testament closes in a solemn atmosphere. From the time of Malachi, the last prophetic voice of the Old Testament, to the birth of Jesus, no divine revelation was given, hence the name, 400 silent years. However, divine providence was still at work during the 400 years between the Testaments. God was setting the stage for the coming of the long-awaited Messiah.

In 336 B.C. Alexander the Great came roaring across Asia Minor, smashed Medo-Persia, and went on to conquer the world for Greece. The Greek language and culture then spread throughout the world. In Egypt the Old Testament was eventually translated into Greek, especially for the many Jews who now no longer read Hebrew. In God's providence, this "Septuagint" version opened God's Word to the entire Graeco-Roman world in the common Greek language of the day, and also prepared the way for the New Testament to be written in this common Greek "world language" of the day.

Symbols for Periods Nine and Ten

Since the information for period ten is brief, we are considering it along with period nine. First, review the symbol at the beginning of the chapter that identifies period nine. Then memorize the added items (on the symbol at the left) that will enable you to recall the key words of period nine. Name the key words:

R _____ from P _____ ;

Z _____ —T _____ ;

E _____ —P _____ ;

N _____ —W _____ ;

E _____ —P _____ .

The "P" and arrow represent RETURN FROM PERSIA. The letters Z-E-N-E represent the four major personalities. Think of this as the last ZENE (scene!) of the Old Testament drama. Each of the four drawings represents the main accomplishment of the person. Note that three (Temple, person, wall) are in the rectangle, and represent accomplishments in Jerusalem. The gallows represents Esther's accomplishments from Persia. The additional key words are ZERUBBABEL—TEMPLE; EZRA—PEOPLE; NEHEMIAH—WALL; and ESTHER—PROTECTION.

Now, cover up the preceding material and then draw the complete symbol. Also, write the name of the period, the Bible location, and each of the key words:

Complete symbol	Period name: _____
	Bible location: _____
	Key words:
	_____ from _____
	_____ — _____
	_____ — _____
	_____ — _____
	_____ — _____

Now review the symbol for period ten above. The rectangle is now broken to form brackets, representing the silent years. Cover up the symbol, then draw it from memory below. Now place the number 400 within the brackets to represent the number of years of this period. For simplicity, we may refer to this period as: **400 SILENT YEARS.**

Complete symbol	Period name: _____

10

PERIOD ELEVEN:
CHRIST

The Cross is the symbol for the eleventh period which is given the title, **CHRIST**. The times were ripe politically, culturally, socially, morally, and religiously for the coming of Christ. Paul wrote about Christ's birth, "But when the time had fully come, God sent his Son" (Gal. 4:4). The world desperately needed the Babe of Bethlehem, who was God in human flesh.

The Four Gospels

The story of the life of Christ is presented in the **FOUR GOSPELS**: Matthew, Mark, Luke, and John. Though all four Gospels deal with Christ's earthly life and ministry—His teachings, miracles, and His death and resurrection each present a different picture of our Lord.

MATTHEW presents Christ as the King and writes primarily to the Jews.

MARK writes to the Romans and presents Christ as the obedient servant.

LUKE depicts Christ as the perfect Son of Man and writes primarily to the Greeks.

JOHN portrays Jesus as the Son of God. He presents to all, especially believers, Christ as personal Savior.

Matthew: King

MATTHEW wrote primarily to show that Jesus was the KING whom the prophets foretold. Matthew also serves as a bridge between the two Testaments. Since his gospel was written to the Jews, it is filled with quotations from the Old Testament (52 citations and 72 additional allusions).

Matthew introduces the King by announcing His royal genealogy, birth, the visit of the Magi, and Jesus' forerunner, John the Baptist. Jesus' baptism and temptation follow in Matthew 4. The King's subjects are described, and the laws of the Kingdom are given, in chapters 5—7. The King's power is displayed through His miracles in chapters 8 and 9, and His ambassadors are commissioned and granted power to exercise His authority in chapter 10. The King's program is revealed in His responses to various groups in chapters 11 and 12 and the growth of His Kingdom is predicted through parables in chapter 13.

Growing opposition creates a crisis in His kingdom, and He predicts His death, and the glory to follow, in Matthew 14—17. Personnel problems among His followers become evident through His discourses on greatness and forgiveness, chapter 18. Further conflict in His Kingdom is seen in questions, debates, and in the final encounters with His enemies, chapters 19—25.

The book climaxes with the death and resurrection of the King in chapters 26—28 and closes with the King's final order. What was that order? (28:18-20)

Mark: Servant

What was MARK's major emphasis in writing about the life of Christ? (10:45)

That Mark wrote for Roman readers is generally agreed. He tells what Jesus did as the humble but perfect SERVANT of God.

It's not surprising therefore that Mark does not include the circumstances of Jesus' birth or genealogy, such as Matthew included. After all, one is more interested in a servant's performance than in his pedigree! Only in Mark are we told that Jesus was a carpenter. Mark moves rapidly through the Servant's life, giving us an orderly account of Jesus' actions. *Euthos*, the Greek word for "immediately" is used 42 times in Mark, and is a servant's word. Twenty miracles are found in Mark, more than in any other gospel, and fewer teachings and parables are found. The Servant works! Mark emphasized Christ's activity, power, and authority. The miracles of Jesus were proofs of His mission from God.

Luke: Son of Man

LUKE was a Greek doctor who traveled extensively with Paul in his ministry. His gospel is a reflection of Paul's teaching—just as Mark's Gospel is a reflection of Peter's teaching. Luke wrote primarily for Gentiles. This comes through in his explanations of Jewish customs and, at times, his substitution of Greek for Hebrew names.

Christ's favorite title for Himself was SON OF MAN. The term is used 26 times in Luke, and shows Jesus' identification with humanity. It reminds us of Jesus' humanity, just as "Son of God" reminds us of His Deity. This gospel presents Christ as the perfect Man, the Savior of imperfect men and women.

In the Book of Luke, Christ is proclaimed as the Savior of all people. He came "to seek and to save" the lost (Lk. 19:10). This is the gospel for outcasts and sinners. Notice that Matthew presents the commission of the Twelve to preach to the Israelites (Mt. 10), whereas Luke presents the sending forth of the seventy to preach to all peoples (Lk. 10). The three parables of "lost things" in chapter 15 teach us of Christ's joy over sinners who repent. The worldwide character of Christianity is portrayed.

In keeping with the emphasis on Christ's humanity, Luke is the only gospel that shows us a glimpse of Christ's childhood. Women and children play a significant role. There is sympathy with the poor and hungry. Luke alone tells us of the shepherds and the birth in the stable. He alone gives us the Good Samaritan, the prodigal son, the tax collector, and the thief on the cross. Luke presents more details about the healing ministry of Jesus than any of the other Gospels.

John: Son of God

The first three Gospels are quite similar. They go together and for this reason are often called the Synoptic Gospels. The Gospel of JOHN stands apart from these first three Gospels in two important ways: First, in content. According to B. F. Westcott, about 92% of the material in John's Gospel is not included in the synoptics. Second, in time. John wrote near the end of the first century, nearly a generation after the other gospel writers. What special reason did John have for selecting the material included in his gospel? (Jn. 20:31)

Interestingly, much of this material fits into groups of seven, all focusing on the fact that Jesus is the SON OF GOD, the Savior of the world. Complete the following:

Seven witnesses in John's Gospel declared Jesus to be "the Son of God." Their names are:

1:32-34 _____   1:49 _____

6:68, 69 _____   10:34-36 _____

11:24-27 _____   20:28 _____

20:30, 31 _____

Seven miracles were signs that "revealed his glory" and led men and women to believe in Him (2:11). The miracles are:

2:1-11 _____

4:45-54 _____

5:1-16 _____

6:1-14 _____

6:15-21 _____

9:1-41 _____

11:1-44 _____

These seven miracles show, respectively, that Jesus, the Son of God, is the Master of quality, distance, time, quantity, natural law, misfortune, and death.

Seven "I am"s of Christ express vital truths about who He was. In each of the following "I am" passages, write down a personal spiritual truth or application.

"I am the bread of life" (6:35).

_____

"I am the light of the world" (8:12).

_____

"I am the gate for the sheep" (10:7).

_____

"I am the good shepherd" (10:11).

_____

"I am the resurrection and the life" (11:25).

_____

"I am the way and the truth and the life" (14:6).

_____

"I am the true vine" (15:1).

_____

Jesus specifically identified Himself with the eternal God, who called Himself the great "I AM" (see Ex. 3:13, 14; Jn. 8:56-58).

Learning from Jesus

Jesus is the world's greatest teacher. We can and ought to spend a lifetime learning from Him. In this lesson we will just touch on a few key lessons from each of the four Gospels that Jesus would teach us.

MATTHEW. Christ asks the same question of His disciples today: "Who do you say I am?" (Mt. 16:15). Record your personal affirmation of who Christ is and what He means to you.

_____

_____

In what areas of life are we to implement the principle set forth in Matthew 6:33? Record past experiences or future plans.

_____

_____

_____

_____

MARK teaches us that joy and fulfillment are found in serving others. Read Mark 9:33-37, an important passage for those who want to work in Christ's Kingdom. How does this incident relate to your service for Christ?

_____

LUKE emphasizes prayer and the Holy Spirit, showing humanity's dependence on God. Fifteen times Christ is seen praying in the Gospels; 11 of these are recorded in Luke.

What do the following passages teach you about the importance of prayer in your ministry: Luke 5:15, 16;

6:11-13; 9:28; 11:1; 18:1-8; and 22:40-46?

_____

_____

_____

_____

JOHN'S Gospel is often used to help people see their spiritual need and how to receive Jesus as Savior and Lord.

From the following passages, jot down important aspects of truth which are important for you to share with a friend who is not yet a Christian.

John 1:10-12 _____

John 3:1-3 _____

John 3:16-18 _____

John 3:19-21 _____

Symbol for Period Eleven

Take a moment to review the basic symbol found at the beginning of this chapter. Then, memorize the added items (on the symbol at the left) that will enable you to recall the key words of this period. Can you name the key words?

M _____ —K _____ ;

M _____ —S _____ ;

L _____ —S _____ of M _____ ;

J _____ —S _____ of G _____ .

Follow the symbols on the cross from top to bottom, then from left to right: MATTHEW—KING; MARK—SERVANT; LUKE—SON OF MAN; JOHN—SON OF GOD. Remember that "King" was written at the top of the cross. The foot of the cross, where Christ's feet were nailed, represents Christ's servanthood—"He went about doing good." The arms of the cross represent His dual nature: on the one hand He was the Son of Man, and on the other hand He was the Son of God.

Cover up the preceding material and then draw the complete symbol. Also, write the name of the period, the Bible location, and each of the key words:

Complete symbol	Period name: _____
	Bible location: _____
	Key words:

_____ — _____

_____ — _____

_____ — _____ of _____

_____ — _____ of _____

11

PERIOD TWELVE:
CHURCH
PART I

 You're coming down the home stretch now. You have almost completed your survey of Bible history. Period 12 will be divided between two lessons: Part I—The Acts, and Part II—The Epistles. The symbol for this period is a church building, and the name of the period is CHURCH.

What did Jesus tell His disciples that He would build? (Mt. 16:18)

What would its purpose be? (Mt. 28:19, 20; Acts 1:8)

The Church is central in God's plan for this age. It is His channel for discipling the world for Christ.

The word for "church" (*ekklesia*) in the New Testament never means a building. What does it mean? (Acts 8:1; 14:27; 18:22)

Check out the following uses of the word "church." Do they refer to a worldwide body or to a local entity of believers? (I Cor. 1:2; Col. 4:15; I Thess. 1:1)

Now do the same with the following passages: Matthew 16:18; I Cor. 12:27, 28; Ephesians 5:25. Do they refer to a worldwide body or to a local entity of believers?

These passages teach that the Church is the worldwide body of all believers, and that it functions in the New Testament as local groups of believers. List the major areas of ministry in which the early church participated. (Acts 2:42)

Acts

The Book of ACTS was written by Luke, Paul's co-laborer, during Paul's first imprisonment in Rome. Acts provides the historical link that connects the four Gospels with the other apostolic writings found in the New Testament.

In Acts we see the beginning of the fulfillment of Christ's plan for the world. Acts shows how the Church became Christ's witness to the world. (The word "witness" is used over 30 times in Acts.) A true church is a witnessing church, and every Christian is called to be a witness. Acts reveals what a New Testament church should provide, what Christian fellowship should be like, and how missionary work should be carried out.

The great pivotal events in the Book of Acts are: the baptism of the Spirit at Pentecost (chap. 2); the persecution of the early church (8:1); the conversion of Saul of Tarsus (chap. 9); the breaking down of the wall of partition between Jew and Gentile (chaps. 10 and 15); the organization of foreign missionary work by the church at Antioch (13:1-3) and the invasion of Europe with the Gospel under Paul (chap. 16).

Pentecost

The disciples of Christ were overjoyed by the reality of His resurrection. With exuberant praise and unshakable conviction they were ready to proclaim the Good News of salvation. But first, Christ had told them, they must wait in Jerusalem until the Holy Spirit came upon them (Acts 1:4, 8). After Jesus ascended (Acts 1:9), the disciples returned to Jerusalem where they waited for the coming of the Comforter. They were now 120 in number, and Matthias was chosen to take Judas's place with the Twelve (Acts 1:15-26).

The Christian Church officially began during the Feast of PENTECOST, when the Holy Spirit descended upon the disciples, accompanied by the symbols of the sound of wind and tongues of fire (Acts 2). The Spirit came to indwell every believer, and to empower them for service. They were enabled to preach with power and in the different languages represented. As Peter proclaimed the meaning of this great event, three thousand people were converted. These converts had come from many parts of the Roman Empire to attend the Jewish Feast of Pentecost. As they returned to their homes they carried with them the glorious news of the Messiah's coming.

Peter: Jews

The apostle PETER was the main spokesman for Christ in Acts 1—12. His ministry was almost exclusively to the JEWS. Other key witnesses during this time were the apostles, James the brother of Christ, Stephen, and Philip.

God used Peter to open the door to the Gentiles in his witness to the household of Cornelius (Acts 10). When Peter explained to the brethren in Jerusalem the reception of Gentiles into the Church, they praised God, saying, "So then, God has granted even the Gentiles repentance unto life" (Acts 11:18). The Gospel spread rapidly and many other Gentiles accepted the

Lord. A large church body developed in Antioch, the capital of the Roman province of Syria (11:19-26). This church became the hub of non-Jewish (or Gentile) Christianity.

Paul: Gentiles

Saul, the persecutor of the church, later became PAUL the great missionary to the GENTILES (Gal. 2:7, 8). The story of his conversion is one of the most thrilling accounts in history (Acts 9:1-9). The foreign missionary activity of the early church is focused in Paul's unparalleled missionary labors (Acts 13—28).

First: Galatia

Paul's FIRST missionary journey, Acts 13, 14, centered in the region of GALATIA, where he established churches in each major city.

Second: Europe

During a year's stay in Antioch, Paul attended the Council of Jerusalem (Acts 15:1-35). Then he took his SECOND missionary journey. While in Asia, he responded to a call from Macedonia and there began his ministry in EUROPE. His longest stay during the second journey was 18 months, in Corinth.

Third: Asia

On his THIRD journey (Acts 18:23—21:4), Paul concentrated on ASIA Minor. During this journey he spent three years in Ephesus.

Fourth: Rome

When Paul returned to Jerusalem, following the third missionary journey, he was arrested and imprisoned for two years (Acts 21:15—26:32). Then he was taken by Roman soldiers on his FOURTH journey, to ROME, Acts 27, 28. There he stayed under guard in a rented house for two years.

Paul was released to resume his missionary activity, then was imprisoned again, and martyred, in 64 A.D. Peter probably was martyred around the same time.

Learning How Churches Grow

In today's lesson we want to learn how Paul started churches and helped them grow. Here are some of his principles. In the spaces provided after each one, state how you might apply that particular principle in your ministry or that of your church.

1. Paul was sent out by the church at Antioch and led by the Holy Spirit (Acts 13:1-4).

_____

2. Paul spoke to those whose hearts were prepared to listen to his message. While Paul typically spoke first to the Jews, when they turned against him, he preached to Gentiles who eagerly heard God's Word. (see Acts 13:46-48 and Mt. 22:1-10)

_____

_____

3. Paul based his message upon Scripture, which he regarded as infallible and Christ-centered (Acts 17:2-4; 18:28).

_____

_____

4. Paul's preaching was not ornate, but demonstrated the power of the Holy Spirit (Acts 14:1; I Cor. 2:1-5).

_____

_____

5. Paul boldly confronted evil and wrong beliefs when he encountered them (Acts 13:6-12).

_____

_____

6. Paul adapted his message to the needs of his hearers in order to get their attention and to make his preaching more effective. (see Acts 17:22, 23; I Cor. 9:19-23)

_____

_____

7. Paul was careful to follow up his converts and establish them in the faith. (Acts 14:21, 22; 15:36)

_____

_____

8. Paul was straightforward in his teaching about the costs of discipleship (Acts 14:21, 22).

_____

_____

9. Paul organized converts into churches and appointed responsible leadership for the work (Acts 14:23; Titus 1:5).

_____

_____

10. Paul promoted a team ministry by training and involving others in the work (Acts 15:40—16:3; 19:9b, 10).

_____

_____

11. Paul ministered primarily in key centers, from there the Gospel spread through trained disciples (Acts 19:1, 10, 20).

_____

_____

Symbol for Period Twelve

Take a moment to review the basic symbol found at the beginning of this chapter. Then, memorize the added

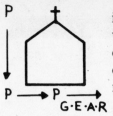

items (on the symbol at the left) that will enable you to recall the key words of Part I of this period, the period covered in the Acts. You should be able to name the key words:

P _____

P _____ —J _____

P _____ —G _____

1—G _____ 2—E _____

3—A _____ 4—R _____

As there were three P's in the launching of Israel in the period of the Exodus, there are three P's that launch the church: **PENTECOST**, **PETER**, and **PAUL**. **PETER** was the Apostle to the **JEWS** and Paul was the Apostle to the **GENTILES**. The first letters of the focal points of Paul's four journeys form an acrostic: G-E-A-R (We might say that Paul was "in gear" in his ministry): **1—GALATIA**, **2—EUROPE**; **3—ASIA**, **4—ROME**.

Cover up the page above and draw the complete symbol for Part I of Period Twelve. Also complete the name of the period, the Bible reference, and each of the key words:

Complete symbol	Period name: _____
	Bible location: _____
	Key words:
	_____
	_____ — _____
	_____ — _____
	1— _____ 2— _____
	3— _____ 4— _____

PERIOD TWELVE:
CHURCH
PART II

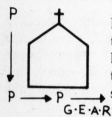

Lesson 11 covered the historical side of the Church period as narrated in the Book of Acts. This final lesson covers the teachings of the Church, as presented in the Epistles and Revelation.

Epistles: Application

The **EPISTLES** (letters) are divided into: 1) the Pauline Epistles, written by Paul, and 2) the General Epistles, written by other apostles. These authoritative letters were written to various church communities and individuals during the early years of the Church. They addressed various needs in the churches, giving Christian truth and the **APPLICATION** of that truth to life.

A major teaching from each of the epistles is covered in this lesson. Don't try to complete all of these studies, however. Instead, focus your study time on one, or perhaps two of them. Be prepared to share the results of your study during the next group meeting.

The Pauline Epistles

ROMANS is a comprehensive presentation of God's plan of redemption. In it, Paul first spoke decisively about the sinfulness of all humankind, chapters 1—3; then he went on to show that all can be justified by faith, in chapter 4. The results of justification, and how to live in Christ are then covered in chapters 5—8. Paul dealt with the matter of general Jewish unbelief in chapters 9—11. He concludes in chapters 12—16 with many practical applications of truth for daily living.

Reflect on the major themes from Romans as they relate to your service for Christ. Why is it so important to first lay the foundation of the great twin truths: our value as created beings loved by the Creator (Rom. 1:7; 8:28-39); and our (humanity's) subsequent fall into sin (Rom. 1:18—3:20)?

_____

_____

Why is the truth that we are justified by faith so essential?

_____

Why is the message of chapters 5—8 of particular importance to you personally?

_____

In what way is Romans 12—16 a good example for our own approach to teaching?

_____

In I CORINTHIANS, Paul responded to errors of personal conduct and doctrine. One of these concerned the believer's resurrection. Make a brief study of this subject from I Corinthians 15 and be prepared to report your findings to your group.

_____

_____

_____

_____

_____

_____

_____

_____

In II Corinthians, Paul was forced to defend his apostleship because various false apostles sought to undermine his authority. He also wanted the church to participate in an offering for the needy Christians in Jerusalem. What principles about giving can you glean from II Corinthians 8 and 9?

_____

_____

_____

Galatians affirms that salvation is solely by grace through faith. Notice how Paul deals with this issue in 3:11-14; 3:23-25; and 5:1-4. Are you aware of the problem of legalism in modern-day church groups? How could you use this epistle to help correct it?

_____

_____

The main doctrinal purpose of Paul's Letter to the Ephesians is to show that all Christians, both Jews and Gentiles, are one in the Body of Christ. The second half of Ephesians is filled with practical applications and admonitions. Unity is an important issue in the Church today. What kind of unity was Paul speaking about? How is this unity expressed in practical terms?

_____

_____

_____

_____

Paul wrote Philippians from prison. In this letter he exhorted his children in the faith to walk with God. It is a letter of great warmth and joy. Note how the theme of

the living Christ in the believer's life is developed in
1:20, 21 and 2:3-18.

_____

_____

_____

_____

COLOSSIANS deals with major doctrinal errors related to
the all-sufficiency of Jesus Christ. Jot down those verses
from Colossians 2:9-17 that are of particular importance
in setting forth Christ's all-sufficiency.

_____

_____

A major doctrinal concern in both I AND II THESSA-
LONIANS is the Second Coming of Christ. Summarize
Paul's teaching on this topic from I Thess. 4—5, and
II Thess. 2. Then, from I Thess. 3:12, 13; 4:1-12; 5:12-28,
make a few notes on how Paul relates this glorious
future event to living here and now.

_____

_____

_____

_____

_____

_____

Paul wrote two letters to his longtime co-worker TIMO-
THY, and one to TITUS. In these letters he warned about
the evils of his day, and gave instructions about leading
their work for God. Read I Timothy 3, and note leadership characteristics important in your service for God.

_____

_____

_____

Paul also wrote a brief letter to PHILEMON on behalf of Onesimus, his runaway slave.

The General Epistles.

HEBREWS was written to struggling Jewish believers who were under strong pressure to abandon their faith in Jesus.

The preeminence of Christ as God and Savior is seen throughout Hebrews. He is set forth both as the great high priest and the final sacrifice for sin. Laced throughout are frequent warnings not to neglect or abandon faith. How is the superiority of Christ seen in each of the following passages?

1:1-4 _____

3:2-6 _____

5:1-10 _____

8:6,7, 13 _____

9:11; 24, 25 _____

10:1-14 _____

JAMES is concerned with how Christianity works in everyday experience. Explain his teaching on the relationship between faith and works in James 2:14-26 in light of Romans 4.

_____

_____

_____

_____

_____

I PETER was written at a time when the dark clouds of persecution were thickening and the lightning arm of Rome was beginning to strike out at God's children. Knowing how to live in times of persecution may not be a pleasant topic, yet it is an important one. Prepare your study, based on I Peter 1:6-9; 2:19-24; 3:13-17; 4:12-19; and 5:8, 9. Describe the general themes of I Peter.

_____

_____

_____

_____

_____

_____

The purpose of II PETER is primarily to combat false teachers whose lives and teachings were licentious. Reflect on Peter's teaching in chapter 2 and note how this teaching is relevant today.

_____

_____

I JOHN provides assurance of the believer's salvation (5:13). Identify the evidences John gives for being sure that you are saved.

2:3-6 _____

2:9-11; 3:14 _____

2:18, 19 _____

2:29; 3:10 _____

3:24; 4:13 _____

5:4, 5 _____

5:10-13 _____

II JOHN and III JOHN are brief letters. II John warns against deceivers and III John encourages the support of true Christian workers.

JUDE warns against apostasy and false doctrine and exhorts us to contend for the true faith. What is the believer's responsibility in the face of widespread apostasy? (Jude 17-23)

John: Culmination

The last book of the New Testament is a special prophecy that JOHN received during his imprisonment on the island of Patmos. It tells of the CULMINATION of world history. It previews the ultimate conquest of evil and the final triumph of the Lord and His people over the forces of Satan. It describes the awesome events on earth just before, during, and after the return of the Lord to this earth. Our Lord Jesus Christ is the exalted one of the Revelation. In this "revelation of Jesus Christ," God's eternal purpose for the world will be completed.

Revelation 4—22 presents the climactic events at the end of world history: the great tribulation (7:14), Armageddon and the Second Coming of Christ (16:16; 19:11-21), the millennial reign of Christ (20:1-6), the final doom of Satan (20:7-10), the great white throne of judgment (20:11-15), the eternal state with the new Heaven and earth (21—22).

Symbol for Period Twelve

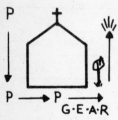

Take a moment to review the basic symbol found at the beginning of this chapter. Then, memorize the added items (on the symbol at the left) that will enable you to recall the key words that have been added in this lesson. Write those words here:

E _____ - A _____

J _____ - C _____

The mailbox represents the EPISTLES, which deal with the APPLICATION of the Gospel in the Church and the life of the Christian. The arrow pointing upward represents the aged apostle JOHN who wrote the final book that points to the CULMINATION of God's redemptive program on earth, including the resurrection of Christians.

Cover up the top of this page and draw the complete symbol for period twelve (including parts I and II). Also write the name of the period, the Bible location, and each of the key words.

Complete symbol	Period name: _____
	Bible location: _____
	Key words:
	_____ - _____
	_____ - _____

Congratulations! You have completed a substantive overview of the entire Bible. The final review on the following pages will help you "nail down" the material you have learned over the past 12 weeks. Fill in the symbols and key words for each of the twelve periods. Feel free to review all of this material before taking this test.

Period One:

Complete symbol	Period name: _____
	Bible location: _____
	Key words:
	_____
	_____
	_____
	_____

Period Two:

Complete symbol	Period name: _____
	Bible location: _____
	Key words:
	_____
	_____
	_____
	_____

Period Three:

Complete symbol	Period name: _____
	Bible location: _____
	Key words:
	_____
	_____
	_____
	_____
	_____
	_____
	_____
	_____

Period Four:

Complete symbol	Period name: _____
	Bible location: _____
	Key words:
	_____
	_____
	_____
	_____ & _____

Period Five:

Complete symbol	Period name: _____
	Bible location: _____
	Key words:
	_____
	_____
	_____
	_____
	_____
	_____
	_____
	_____

Period Six:

Complete symbol

Period name: _____

Bible location: _____

Key words:

_____ — _____

_____ — _____

_____ — _____

_____ — _____

_____   _____

_____

Period Seven:

Complete symbol

Period name: _____

Bible location: _____

Key words:

_____ = _____

_____

_____ = _____

_____ , _____

_____

Period Eight:

| Complete symbol | Period name: _____ |
| Bible location: _____ |
| Key words: |
| _____ — _____ |
| _____ ; |
| _____ — _____ |
| _____ |

Period Nine:

| Complete symbol | Period name: _____ |
| Bible location: _____ |
| Key words: |
| _____ from _____ |
| _____ — _____ |
| _____ — _____ |
| _____ — _____ |
| _____ — _____ |

Period Ten:

| Complete symbol | Period name: _____ |

Period Eleven:

Complete symbol

Period name: _____

Bible location: _____

Key words:

_____ — _____

_____ — _____

_____ — _____ of _____

_____ — _____ of _____

Period Twelve, Part I:

Complete symbol

Period name: _____

Bible location: _____

Key words:

_____

_____ — _____

_____ — _____

1— _____   2— _____

3— _____   4— _____

Period Twelve, Part II:

Complete symbol

Period name: _____

Bible location: _____

Key words:

_____ — _____

_____ — _____

This LAMP course is designed to be a tool you can use to help others know and experience the truth of God's Word as well. Here are a few suggestions for how you might share this course with others.

1. Plan "family devotionals" covering one period each week. This can be a special time, in which each family member draws the completed symbol, sharing its main truths, and applies a major theme from that period.

2. You might plan to work through these lessons with a friend, covering one lesson each week. Your friend should have a copy of the book, and you should have a copy of the Leader's Guide.

3. Some of you will want to lead another class through this material, possibly in much the same way as you went through it in your group. It is not necessary to "know all the answers" in order to lead a study group over this course. If you prepare your lesson well and afresh, and use the study guide appropriately, you can have a successful class.

Take time now to think of ways you could share the truths you have learned in this course. Write these thoughts below, and be prepared to talk about them in your final group session.

_____

_____

_____

_____

_____

LESSON PLANS

Groups differ greatly in terms of how they like to structure themselves and go about the learning process. Some groups will simply want to "stick to the facts" without much personal interaction. Other groups will want to focus almost exclusively on intimate sharing and application of the lesson.

Time is also a factor. You may find that your group can function quite well by simply going over the answers to workbook questions, having prayer and a short time of fellowship. Other groups may want to spend much more time with a detailed lesson plan. So consider the lesson plan activities below as *suggestions only*. Use what you can, but feel free to skip portions or rearrange the order to fit your group's needs.

Important Notes

- This guide will focus students' attention upon the overall general theme of each lesson. Details should be covered as you go over the filled-out workbooks together, and discuss students' answers.

- Look through all of these lessons to note places where advanced preparation is needed, or materials must be gotten well before the class session. That way you won't be caught off guard.

- Try to include in all your group sessions some of the

key ingredients for building group life: a time for sharing, a time for prayer, and perhaps light refreshments around which significant conversation can take place. Bible study groups can be much more than just an intellectual exercise. They can become a means of developing strong bonds of Christian fellowship.

- Have an informal Introductory Meeting before jumping right into the study. This meeting should include: plenty of time to get acquainted with each other, time to get acquainted with the LAMP course in general, time to hand out the books and give clear instructions about what will be expected each week (but give an *ending date*, too). Be sure to start building into the group a sense of accountability for one another.

During the Introductory Meeting you will need to go over the main goal for the *Panorama of the Bible* course: to grasp the basic idea of each symbol and how it illustrates what was happening during that Bible period—to learn the symbol and related key ideas for that period. The lessons will also raise questions and provide study projects that involve the learner in his or her own study of Scripture. Learners should write answers in their workbooks, and jot down questions or mark unclear passages to bring up in class.

- In advance, prepare poster boards with each of the 12 symbols drawn on them. Sometime **at the beginning or end of each class session,** you should take a few moments to display the symbols learned in the previous lessons, one at a time, going over each element point by point in order to reinforce the symbols in your students' memories. (As an alternative, ask volunteers to explain the symbols as you display them.)
- The Discover section will usually highlight the general theme of the lesson, found near the end of each chapter (under the "Learning About" heading). It will get students into the Bible with an exercise to help reinforce the application of this general theme.

In the Discover section, students will have a chance to discuss items from their workbooks that puzzled or interested them in their personal study. A general piece of advice is in order here. Don't read through the workbook item by item and answer by answer. That approach provides no challenge to your students; in fact, it makes it easy for them to "fake it" by simply looking over the material in class and coming up with an answer off the "tops of their heads." To prevent this, let them know from the first that you expect that they'll do their work before class. As you come to a section of the workbook, ask for general comments or questions that might have surfaced in their individual study. Then ask a discussion question or two to further stimulate their thinking.

To close each Discover section (or as part of the Discuss section) of the class time: 1.) Always ask for any questions/observations/sharing from the workbook assignment during the week. 2.) Go over the answers to specific key questions in the chapter. 3.) Be sure to have a "symbol review" in which students practice drawing the symbols, checking their progress in memorizing them. **These three steps should be done each week— EVEN THOUGH THEY WILL NOT BE MENTIONED EACH TIME IN THE SPECIFIC LESSON PLANS.**

Lesson 1

Focus: Give each person a small index card as he or she enters the room. Begin the session with an introduction like this: "Some of you may have studied your genealogies. Others may have just heard parents and relatives talking about your ancestors. On your card, write the name of the earliest direct ancestor you know about, and the approximate year when he or she was born."

Have volunteers read the names and dates on their cards. Ask whether they know anything at all about what their ancestors were like. Then ask: "Do you, or any of your relatives, have those same characteristics?"

At this point announce that, just as it sometimes helps to understand a person by knowing his ancestors, so we can better understand all human beings by going back to the very beginning of human history. Today's lesson will be about several "first causes," and an understanding of these causes can help us deal with the effects we see in our world today.

DISCOVER: One of the key topics in this lesson is the advent and universality of sin—and its judgment by God. Spend some time dealing with the subject of temptation. Read Genesis 3:6 with I John 2:16, and list on the board the three aspects of temptation. Then divide into groups of three. The groups will brainstorm answers to: "In what ways are people today (in my society, community, workplace, family) most tempted in regard to each of the three areas?" Answers should be specific examples, though the level of personal sharing is up to the groups.

Reassemble the whole group and list answers under each of the three headings. Discuss: "In what practical ways can we as Christians deal with these temptations?" Find Scripture that lends encouragement.

DISCUSS: In your opinion, what does it mean to be created in the image of God? What affect does this have upon your own personal self-image? Give a practical example.

RESPOND: As we prepare to meet the needs of other people, it is important to realize that most human hurts result from the effects of sin. Encourage each class member to think of a specific person who has a need. Ask each student to write that person's name somewhere private (perhaps in their workbook) and commit to pray for that person every day this coming week.

Lesson 2

FOCUS: In your own words, tell the following story: A man was boarding an airliner for his first flight. He worriedly calculated the weight of the passengers and concluded, "This plane will never get off the ground." But he determined to do what he could to help.

As the jet took off, he held tightly to his seat arms, pulling upward as hard as he could. When the plane banked to the left, he pulled up on the right arm and pushed down on the left. When the plane hit an air pocket, he pulled up until the plane leveled off again. When an updraft made the craft lift slightly, he gently pushed down with his hands.

Eventually they landed at their destination. As the plane came to a stop at the terminal, the man slowly relaxed his hands and collapsed back into his seat, soaked with sweat. The woman next to him, who had noticed his tenseness during the flight, remarked, "I think that was a very good flight."

With an exhausted smile, the man looked up and said, "Thank you."

Lead a short discussion of the story with the following questions: 1) Why was this man so miserable? 2) What should he have done?

Help students make the transition to today's lesson by reminding them of what they learned last week. Some Christians are confused about the true source of their salvation. They think faith isn't enough; instead they are tempted to rely on faith *plus* something—baptism, good works, church attendance, etc.

This lesson will help students see, from the lives of four patriarchs, that the only possible connecting link for our relationship with God is faith.

DISCOVER: Take some time to do a more in-depth study of Abraham, and the nature of his faith. By two's study the five passages on page 18 giving examples of Abraham's godly character and faith. First let the students answer: What was the basic challenge of faith for Abraham in this situation? What would have been the main temptation that could have kept him from proceeding with faith and obedience?

Then have the participants try to translate Abraham's experience into made-up, modern-day scenarios of faith-building situations comparable to the kinds of faith decisions Abraham successfully faced. For example, where the workbook says: "He left his homeland . . . .", the student might say: "He left Mississippi to go to Chicago to take a job in which he was no longer expected to buy liquor for his sales clients . . ." (let them fill in the details), etc. Share the scenarios and discuss implications.

DISCUSS: Have you, or a Christian you know, ever felt called by God to do something comparable to God's command to Abraham to sacrifice his son Isaac? Share what happened. If you had been Abraham, how do you think you would have responded?

RESPOND: Ask for volunteers to share their personal experience of putting their faith in Christ. How did they come to that point? How has it made a difference?

Close this session by thanking God that our faith in Him gives us hope that enables us to persevere in service, waiting for the Lord to change people in His own time and way.

Lesson 3

FOCUS: Prepare a WET PAINT sign and have it attached to a piece of furniture in the room as participants enter. When the class begins, ask: "Who (secretly?) touched the 'wet paint'? Who wanted to?"

Then read Romans 7:9, 10. Discuss the law as a stumbling block. Say: "Share an experience in which the 'rules' seemingly caused you to break them. How would you describe your actions in light of Romans 7?"

DISCOVER: Have a Bible verse search contest. Hand out sheets of paper with the Ten Commandments listed in one column and another column with the heading: "New Testament Restatement." Have participants see who can find a New Testament restatement for all of the Ten Commandments first. (Make a Bible Concordance available.) Spend time talking about the different motive for obeying these New Testament principles.

DISCUSS: In what situations have you had the opportunity to witness the "Caleb and Joshua type" of faith? In what areas of your own life do you wish you had more such faith? Share.

RESPOND: Close by having the first "symbol review test." Have students put away their workbooks, and distribute sheets of paper photocopied from pages 103 and 104 at the back of the book. Students are to draw, as quickly as possible, the complete symbols for periods 1, 2, and 3. They must supply the period name, Bible location, and key words for each symbol.

Lesson 4

FOCUS: Ask participants to think back to when they were about ten years old. Ask them who their heroes were then. When a student gives the name of a hero, ask: "Why was that person your hero?"

When several have said something about their childhood heroes, say something about the effect heroes have on us. We daydream about them. We take them as our example, adopting their standards and values. Our goal is to be like them. Then mention that Bible characters can play a similar role for us. God often uses the Bible biographies of godly men and women to stimulate us to greater spiritual maturity. This lesson features such a personality. His name is Joshua.

DISCOVER: Ask students to share answers from the character analysis of Joshua, page 38. To make sure everyone contributes, let each person contribute only one characteristic until all others have suggested answers. As students respond, write their answers on the board.

When the picture is as complete as it's going to get, ask them to discuss this issue: "What would our church

116

be like if everyone in it looked to Joshua as a role model and aspired to have these personal traits?" Explore the implications for corporate worship, mutual service, and individual holiness.

DISCUSS: Based on your examination of I Corinthians 12, what effect does an individual's sin have on others in the church? Give some possible examples.

RESPOND: To close the session, divide into groups of 2 or 3 and let students share and pray for each other along these lines: "What are some situations you personally face right now in which you need to have the courage of a hero? Or is there a challenge you face in which you would like to step out and do 'heroic deeds for God'?"

Lesson 5

FOCUS: Write the following sentence on the chalkboard: "If opportunity disguised itself as temptation, it would only *have* to knock once." Ask students to react to it.

Then talk about how attractive temptation can be to us. It doesn't seem to matter whether we've been burned before. Something about our sin nature keeps us from thinking clearly in the presence of an alluring temptation. But the Bible helps us remember what we're prone to forget. Accounts of spiritual failure warn us about the consequences of sin. This lesson contains just that kind of warning.

DISCOVER: Expand on the dual themes of this lesson (temptation and safeguards) by doing a topical Bible study on "Biblical Resources Against Sin." Assign the following verses (and others you may choose) to group members for study: Judges 2:10-23; Mt. 4:1-11; Mt. 5:29, 30; Lk. 14:26-33; Jn. 15:18-21; I Cor. 8:9-13; I Cor. 10:13; II Cor. 6:17, 18; Rom. 8:12, 13, 35-39; Rom. 13:14; Rom. 14:1-22; Col. 3:1-11; Eph. 6:11-15; James 1:13-15; I Pet. 4:1, 2; Rev. 12:10, 11.

Then, on the chalkboard, fill in the outline below

with the accumulated Bible knowledge of the participants as they call out their insights: I. Vault of Resources; II. Role of Temptation; III. Role of Willpower; IV. Role of the Triune God; V. Role of Christian Maturity; VI. Reasons for Encouragement; VI. Promises to Rely On.

DISCUSS: In Judges 6:12 God calls Gideon a "mighty warrior." Surely, at that point, Gideon didn't feel like one. In your opinion, how similar is God's vision of you (from the Scriptures) to your own vision of yourself?

RESPOND: Hand out envelopes with notecards inside them. (The notecards have II Pet. 5:17 written on the back.) Give students directions for an exercise they might want to do at home during a time of being alone with God. Say: "Write your most grievous personal temptation on the notecard. Place it in the envelope, seal it, and address it to God. Then hold the envelope high above your head with both hands, giving this burden to God until you can't hold it up anymore: 'Lord, I can't carry the weight of this burden anymore—You take it.' Then drop your arms. Destroy the envelope. Spend time praising God for his provisions of both strength and forgiveness in the face of temptation. In your future prayers remind yourself that you have cast your cares upon God and that He has promised to take them."

Lesson 6

FOCUS: Begin with a leader-trust exercise. Divide into pairs. One member of each pair is blindfolded and asked to follow his partner around the room (or outside) by being led by the hand—for about five minutes. Then blindfold the other partner and repeat the exercise. (Note: Some may not want to participate. Let them watch and be ready to share their observations later.)

Have a brief discussion about the experience of leading and following. Ask such questions as: How did you feel as you were being led? How much did you trust your partner? Did your trust level increase as time passed? Did you sense that your leader sincerely wanted to keep you from crashing into things? Did you feel he or she had a "good heart"? (good intentions about looking out for you?).

From this, move into the Discover exercise dealing with the "hearts" of Saul, David, Solomon.

DISCOVER: Make three columns on the chalkboard labeled *Saul: Bad Heart/ David: Good Heart/ Solomon: Divided Heart*. Then have participants divide into three groups to search the Scripture (without looking at their workbooks) for information about these three leaders of Israel. Their task is to come up with Scripture passages that confirm the "heart labels" that have been given to these leaders. Come together as a large group to write down this information in the columns.

Now look over the characteristics of the three kinds of leaders and make a modern-day application. Ask: "Can you name an example from your experience at work, in the community, or in world events for each kind of leadership?" Discuss the benefits of being led by a "good heart" leader.

DISCUSS: In light of I Corinthians 1:26-31, share a time when you felt "weak" or "foolish," but God seemed to use you anyway.

RESPOND: Lead your students in a discussion of the leadership needs in your church. Name the heads of committees and boards. Mention others who might have more informal leadership roles. As each is mentioned, ask volunteers to identify items from the list of leadership principles (from David's life, on p. 54 that have application to that leadership position.

Close by having the second "symbol review test." Have students put away their workbooks, and distribute sheets of paper photocopied from pages 105 and 106 at the back of the book. Students are to draw, as quickly as possible, the complete symbols for periods 4, 5, and 6. They must supply the period name, Bible reference, and key words for each symbol.

Lesson 7

FOCUS: Have students react to the following statements from Christian executives about how they lead:

- Sam: I like everyone to have their say. If a good idea surfaces from someone at any level in the company, we'll take a serious look at it. When employees have input, they develop a sense of ownership in the project. It makes for better work and better morale. I've never had any problems sharing the power.

- Martha: As far as I'm concerned, leadership from the top down is the only way to go. It's also the most Biblical—when you consider God's way of leading us. We must trust and obey. With this kind of leadership, I know everything that's going on. Things tend to get messed up unless I'm at the controls. There's also no question about who does what, and when. People feel a lot more comfortable when they know where they stand. Besides, if there's one thing I hate—it's surprises on the job.

- Walter: As a Christian, I honestly don't feel it's my place to give orders. I try to lead by example only. If people follow, fine. Jesus never coerced anyone to follow Him, so how could I feel right about doing it?

Then write the following equation on the chalkboard: LEADER = SERVANT. Ask whether students agree or disagree, and why. Also ask how widespread is the acceptance of this definition. How might a non-Christian person change the equation?

After a few minutes of interaction, tell students that today's lesson continues the story of the monarchy. Therefore, you'll be discussing various personalities again, analyzing them according to the standards found in the Bible.

DISCOVER: Hand out a previously prepared "Interview Outline" sheet to each participant. This will have the following headings with space for writing: 1) Work History; 2) Spiritual IQ and Character Profile; 3) Major Strengths; 4) Major Weaknesses; 5) Work Habits; 6) Servanthood Index; 7) Salary Requirement.

Each Participant will pretend to be a Personnel Manager, interviewing candidates for CEO (Chief Executive Officer) of _____ (name of their own company, club, church, etc.). The candidates' names will be pulled from this group of people studied in the chapter: Ahab (I Ki. 16:29-33), Elijah (I Ki. 18, 19), Elisha (II Ki. 6), Hezekiah (II Ki. 18—20), Josiah (II. Ki. 22, 23), Habbakkuk.

Let students review their candidate's life history—or specific events in their lives—in Scripture, then fill out the outline. Then have them share with the group why they would hire their particular candidate, by relating that person's qualities from the notes on their outline.

DISCUSS: Who is your "Most Unforgettable Character" when it comes to someone who really knew how to lead? Share about that person.

Remember that the ancient kings of Israel were people like us, yet they were responsible for making decisions that affected the welfare and destiny of entire nations. If you were suddenly—miraculously—made President of the United States, what is the first thing you would do about U.S.—Soviet relations? World hunger? The national debt? Other national problems?

RESPOND: Close the class by distributing 3" x 5" cards, one to each student. Ask each student to write on the card one of the characteristics of a godly servant-leader which they want God to develop in their own lives. When all have written on their cards, close the class in prayer, asking God to remind them of what they've written and to give them the strength and determination to develop into godly leaders.

Lesson 8

Focus: Ask participants to pair off with a person sitting next to them. Then ask the pairs to share with each other the most effective punishment they received as children. ("Most effective" means it kept them from repeating the offense.)

After a couple of minutes, ask whether any volunteers would care to reveal their punishments to the whole class. After a few have shared, and the laughter has died down, announce that this lesson deals with the subject of discipline also—but on a national level.

Discover: Divide into two groups and assign each group one of these passages relating to discipline: Hebrews 12:1-13 and John 15:1-8. Each group is to pretend to be a ministerial meeting. The pastors are working together on a sermon outline for the passage. Each sermon should have the following elements:

Title:
Theme:
Key Biblical Truth:
Introduction:
Three points:
Application Point:
Concluding Illustration:

(You may want to have sheets of paper with these headings to hand out to each group member for filling in their ideas.) When the "sermons" are completed have the group choose one of the "pastors" to share their groups' sermon outline.

Discuss: What are some of the benefits of God's discipline? How would you counsel a Christian who interprets every bad thing that happens as a punishment from God?

Respond: Ask students to think about a time when they were disciplined by the Lord. Encourage them to define discipline by the positive effects that came from an experience. Maybe it was a personal hardship or illness, an experience of failure, the heartbreak of a broken relationship. After a few minutes to think of an occasion when they experienced the Lord's discipline, ask if any would like to briefly tell about it—in a very general way. Be ready with an experience of your own to get the sharing going and to set the pattern.

After several have shared such experiences, lead in a prayer of thanksgiving for God's discipline. Thank Him for loving us enough to keep after us until we return in a renewed commitment to Him.

Lesson 9

FOCUS: Have students write their answers to the following sentence starters:

- When faced with a seemingly impossible task, I generally:
- During the times when I have overcome tremendous obstacles, my perseverance was usually due to:
- When I have faced very difficult times, I have found my faith to be:

Let students share, then move to a study of Nehemiah. The major portion of this lesson deals with the return from exile. The Jewish people faced a number of obstacles during this time, and it will be helpful to learn how they overcame those obstacles successfully.

DISCOVER: Focus your study on the section dealing with Nehemiah's methods of handling opposition. Divide into pairs, with each pair taking one or more of the eight instances of opposition and response (p. 77). Have each pair study their passages and present to the group: 1) a summary of the historical opposition and Nehemiah's response; 2) a brief roleplay of a similar modern-day situation of opposition and a possible Christian way of responding to it.

DISCUSS: When dealing with opposition, is there ever a case where it is best to fight back, rather than "turn the other cheek"? Explain. How would you apply your answer to national policy?

RESPOND: Close by having the third "symbol review test." Have students put away their workbooks, and distribute sheets of paper photocopied from pages 106 and 107 at the back of the book. Students are to draw, as quickly as possible, the complete symbols for periods 7, 8, and 9. They must supply the period name, Bible reference, and key words for each symbol.

Note: This is the third review test. You'll notice that each one has gotten a little harder; each one is a little more threatening to your students' egos. By now your message should have gotten across loud and clear—this is important material, and you take it seriously! Remind them that there will be a final test three sessions from now. It will cover all twelve symbols!

Lesson 10

FOCUS: Have the class pretend to be amateur "Gospel marketers." Divide into small groups (or do this individually) and let each take one of the following audiences. They must tell how they would "package" the Gospel message toward each particular type of person.

1. A corporate executives meeting
2. A group of migrant workers
3. Yuppies
4. Homosexuals
5. The Brotherhood of Steelworkers convention
6. A team of nuclear physicists
7. A typical American family
8. A vocal, self-proclaimed atheist
9. A Jewish Old Testament scholar

From this exercise, lead into a brief lecture covering the main points in the lesson on the differences in audience and approach of the four Gospel writers.

DISCOVER: Now zero in on a key passage in John supporting the deity of Christ: John 1:1-14. Have the students do a word study on the Greek word, *logos*. You will need to do some advanced preparation for this. Ask your pastor to loan you the reference tools for the study group to use as you allow them to do some research for themselves. (Make sure you have thoroughly studied the passage and the word *logos* before coming to the class.) Say: "Take about 15 or 20 minutes to study the word *logos*."

The study tools should include such works as:

4 or 5 good commentaries
An exhaustive concordance
A Theological Dictionary of the New Testament.

Reconvene and compare notes, sharing insights from the study time. Relate the discussion to the question: "How would I answer someone who said that Jesus was a great teacher, but merely human like any other great man?"

DISCUSS: The Gospel of John shows the miraculous as a means of leading people to belief. Will a person who has witnessed a divine miracle *always* come to faith in Christ? Explain your answer.

RESPOND: As a means of encouragement concerning the deity of Christ, consider a reading from from C. S. Lewis's book, *Mere Christianity.* Read the last paragraph of the chapter entitled, "The Shocking Alternative." Lead in a prayer of thankfulness for the greatness of our God and Savior, Jesus.

Lesson 11

FOCUS: In groups of four, have participants roleplay and discuss the following case study: They are to be a church board meeting. Present are a new pastor, a long-time member, a new member, and the church treasurer. The pastor announces: "We are meeting tonight to formulate a 1-year, 3-year, and 5-year plan for growing this church." It is an old church averaging 20 attenders on Sunday, all retired except one. There are no programs or Sunday School other than weekly worship services. There is a $250 a week budget. Play the roles. Develop the plan. Share with the group.

DISCOVER: Read this quote from the chapter: "Acts reveals what a New Testament church should provide, what Christian fellowship should be like, and how missionary work should be carried out." With this in mind, focus on a passage indicating important aspects of the early church's fellowship, instruction, worship, and growth: Acts 2:42-47.

Have learners study the passage silently, then write up a document that might be labeled: Declaration of Church Dependence. It will contain a statement of what the learner believes are "the absolute essentials for healthy church life." Hand out sheets of 8 1/2" x 11" paper with this statement: "We hold these truths to be self-evident: That all healthy churches must have": Let learners use this passage to complete their documents. Allow students to bring in other Bible passages, if needed, to round out the picture. Then discuss: In what ways does our church match up? What might we consider adding? AND (more difficult) what might God be calling us to reevaluate or stop doing, that may be hindering our health and/or growth?

DISCUSS: In your opinion, what is the most effective way to "grow a church" in modern America? Why? What evidence do you have? Why do people join your own local church?

RESPOND: Have a brainstorming session. Simply compile ALL ideas about how to encourage growth in your particular church. These would be SPECIFIC programs, ministries, outreach projects, based upon the 11 principles derived from the experience of Paul (pp. 93 and 94). As a group, choose one to pray about, with the goal of sharing the idea with others in the church.

Lesson 12

FOCUS: Ask learners to think back over the past weeks. Then ask this question: How has this course changed your concept of the Bible? Encourage them to use the posted symbols to refresh their memories. After a number have answered, mention that this lesson is intended to pull together all they've studied in a way that will help them be more effective in their ministry to others.

DISCOVER: Give your students a chance to shine. Announce that you're going to call on each learner to share his or her insights from one or more of the Bible passages they studied. Ask them for the important facts they learned. These might include a major theme, or the circumstances that prompted the Bible book's writing, or the effect the author wanted the book to have in the lives of his readers. During this exercise, encourage learners to share their findings directly from their workbooks. Add your own insights from your study as appropriate.

FINAL REVIEW: Your group members have come a long way. And as you post the twelfth symbol alongside the others, the whole scope of what they've covered just might overwhelm them. But don't give them time to feel intimidated. Instead, go right into a review activity that will reinforce what they've learned—and, more important—give them a sense of mastery.

Different activities work better for different classes. You know your students, so pick the one that fits them best. Here are some alternatives:

1. Draw 12 squares on the chalkboard, number them, and ask for volunteers to draw the symbol for each period. When the symbols have been drawn, have each artist supply the following information for his or her symbol: period name, Bible location, and key words.

2. Divide the class into teams. Have each team line up so that every member of each team is directly across from a member of the opposing team. The first one in each line gets a chance at the first question; the two second-in-line students get a crack at the second question, etc. Use a pointer and randomly ask students to identify what you point toward. Or, point to a whole symbol and ask: What period? Which books of the Bible? Point to a specific element and ask: What does this letter stand for? The first of the two players to give the correct answer earns a point for his team.

3. Go through the symbols one by one, in chronological order. As you point to each one, ask volunteers to identify the period, the Bible location, and the key words represented in the symbol.

RESPOND: Ask volunteers to share what they've written in answer to the very last assignment in the workbook. How could they communicate what they've learned in this course? What people need this information? How will this knowledge equip them to be more effective in lay ministry?

The purpose of this activity is to point students toward the future as they finish this course. The course has not been an end in itself; its goal is future service on the part of your students.

Close this class with prayer for your students. If they are open to the idea, ask them to stand in a circle and join hands. They've gone through a lot together; they're no doubt closer to each other now than when the course began. In your prayer, commit your students to God's care as they go out to serve Him.